"The twenty-first century is the century of global Christianity. In this century, we are increasingly aware of the fact that the growth of the Christian faith around the world is the result of obedience in mission on the part of previous generations of Christians. Since God expects all Christians to be about advancing his rule in the world, mission today must become the responsibility of the global church. *The New Global Mission,* written by a person who knows mission from multiple perspectives, is a masterful articulation of the need for mission to be the joyous duty of Christians from everywhere. It is especially useful as a tool for education about mission in diverse Christian settings."

TITE TIÉNOU, ACADEMIC DEAN AND PROFESSOR OF THEOLOGY OF MISSION, TRINITY EVANGELICAL DIVINITY SCHOOL, DEERFIELD, ILLINOIS

"In a truly global perspective, this passionate and yet well-reasoned and eminently readable plea for a holistic mission is a must-read for all who care about the kingdom of God and the transformation of the kingdoms of this world. Writing with knowledge and sensitivity reflective of his worldwide experience, Escobar combines the high idealism of the biblical vision with a sober assessment of political, social, religious and cultural realities of our time. Delightful and challenging at the same time!"

PETER KUZMIČ, DISTINGUISHED PROFESSOR OF WORLD MISSIONS AND EUROPEAN STUDIES, GORDON-CONWELL THEOLOGICAL SEMINARY, AND FOUNDING PRESIDENT OF THE EVANGELICAL THEOLOGICAL SEMINARY IN OSIJEK, CROATIA

"This book is must reading for all those who would lead Christ's church in this new millennium. Two-thirds of all Christians now live in Asia, Africa and Latin America. This means that the church's mission is now a truly global enterprise, as Escobar shows. Samuel Escobar, the dean of Latin American Protestant evangelical missiologists, gives us here an insightful, careful, concise and passionate overview of the complex and constantly changing reality facing us all in the church's mission today. Escobar demonstrates a clear and compelling missionary commitment to the missional goal that, in the words of Donald McGavran, 'women and men become disciples of Jesus Christ and responsible members of Christ's Church.' The book's insightful trinitarian organization is capped off by a very helpful review of selected works by mission thinkers of the past fifty years."

CHARLES VAN ENGEN, ARTHUR F. GLASSER PROFESSOR OF BIBLICAL THEOLOGY OF MISSION, FULLER THEOLOGICAL SEI AND FORMER MISSIONARY TO MEXICO

CHRISTIAN
DOCTRINE
IN GLOBAL
PERSPECTIVE

The New Global Mission

THE GOSPEL FROM EVERYWHERE TO EVERYONE

Samuel Escobar

Series Editor: David Smith
Consulting Editor: John Stott

InterVarsity Press
Downers Grove, Illinois

InterVarsity Press
P.O. Box 1400, Downers Grove, IL 60515-1426
World Wide Web: www.ivpress.com
E-mail: mail@ivpress.com

InterVarsity Press® is the book-publishing division of InterVarsity Christian Fellowship/USA®, a student movement
active on campus at hundreds of universities, colleges and schools of nursing in the United States of America,
and a member movement of the International Fellowship of Evangelical Students. For information about local and
regional activities, write Public Relations Dept., InterVarsity Christian Fellowship/USA, 6400 Schroeder Rd.,
P.O. Box 7895, Madison, WI 53707-7895, or visit the IVCF website at <www.ivcf.org>.

All Scripture quotations, unless otherwise indicated, are taken from the Holy Bible, New International Version®.
NIV®. Copyright ©1973, 1978, 1984 by International Bible Society. Used by permission of Hodder and Stoughton
Ltd. All rights reserved. "NIV" is a registered trademark of International Bible Society. UK trademark number
1448790. Distributed in North America by permission of Zondervan Publishing House.

Cover design: Cindy Kiple

Cover image: Paul and Lindamarie Ambrose/Getty Images

ISBN 0-8308-3301-3

Printed in the United States of America ∞

Library of Congress Cataloging-in-Publication Data

Escobar, Samuel E.
    The new global mission: the Gospel from everywhere to everyone/
Samuel Escobar
        p. cm.—(Christian doctrine in global perspective)
Includes bibliographical references and index.
    ISBN 0-8308-3301-3 (pbk.: alk. paper)
    1. Missions—Theory. I. Title. II. Series.
    BV2063.E79 2003
    266—dc22

                                                                    2003016149

P	17	16	15	14	13	12	11	10	9	8	7	6	5	4	3	2	1
Y	15	14	13	12	11	10	09	08	07	06	05	04	03				

Contents

Series Preface

THIS BOOK IS ONE OF A SERIES TITLED Christian Doctrine in Global Perspective being published by a partnership between Langham Literature and InterVarsity Press. Langham Literature is a program of John Stott Ministries, the U.S. movement within the Langham Partnership International.

The vision for the series has arisen from the knowledge that during the twentieth century a dramatic shift in the Christian center of gravity took place. There are now many more Christians in Africa, Asia and Latin America than there are in Europe and North America. Two major issues have resulted, both of which Christian Doctrine in Global Perspective seeks to address.

First, the basic theological texts available to pastors, students and lay readers in the Southern Hemisphere have for too long been written by Western authors from a Western perspective. What is needed now are more books by non-Western writers that reflect their own cultures. In consequence, this series has an international authorship, and we thank God that he has raised up so many gifted writers from the developing world whose resolve is to be both biblically faithful and contextually relevant.

Second, non-Western authors need to write not only for non-Western readers but for Western readers as well. Indeed, the adjective *global* is intended to express our desire that biblical understanding will flow freely in all directions. Certainly we in the West need to listen to and learn from our sisters and brothers in other parts of the world. And the decay of many Western churches urgently needs an injection of non-Western Christian vitality. We pray that this series will open up channels of communication in fulfillment of the apostle Paul's conviction that it is only *together with all the saints* that we will be able to grasp the dimensions of Christ's love (Eph 3:18).

Never before in the church's long and checkered history has this possibility been so close to realization. We hope and pray that Christian Doctrine in Global Perspective may, in God's good providence, play a part in making it a reality in the twenty-first century.

John R. W. Stott
David W. Smith

Preface

THE TRUTH OF THE GOSPEL THAT GIVES LIFE MEANING is always a word we have received. We do not have it when we come to this world; it is a word someone else passes on to us. And once we have received it we are bound to share it. That privilege and joy is at the heart of Christian mission. Thankfulness is a gift from God that drives us to take our part in what the Spirit is doing in the world: making Christ known and transforming human beings into his likeness.

As I deliver these pages to the readers of this book, I feel it appropriate to thank God for the missionaries who crossed the sea to take the gospel of Jesus Christ to Arequipa in southern Peru, the town where I was born. My father had come to faith through the work of the missionaries from the Evangelical Union of South America, known today as Latin Link. Iza Elder had gone to Peru from New Zealand under that mission. Besides my parents she was the expert teacher who first explained the gospel and the way of true life to me. I want this book to be a tribute to them.

My special thanks go to John Stott who encouraged me to complete this project as we walked in the quiet yard of All Nations Christian College near London and along the busy streets of Lima. Thanks also go to David Smith for his editorial advice. He was an able host at the work-

shop in which the first chapters of this book took final form, and he has
been an encouraging editor along the way.

I am also grateful to Eastern Baptist Theological Seminary for the sab-
batical term that allowed me to complete the project, and to International
Ministries of the American Baptist Churches that support my present missionary work in Spain. I have owed much to InterVarsity Press since my
university days! It is a privilege to have them as my publisher.

Samuel Escobar
Valencia, Spain

1

Christian Mission in a New Century

NOT FAR FROM THE CENTRAL AREA of the German city of Hanover is a Baptist church that houses a Spanish-speaking congregation under the pastoral care of José Antonio González. Like many young people from Spain in the 1960s, José Antonio left his beautiful town in Galicia and emigrated to Germany in search of a job. There he was befriended by Mrs. Pinto, a Bolivian lady whose family had also gone to Germany in search of economic security. She not only provided José Antonio with good spiced soups but also insisted on sharing the gospel of Jesus Christ and praying for him. As a nominal Catholic, José Antonio had never thought that this story, part of the folksong heritage of his native Spain, could have any relevance for an aspiring student of industrial design. Eventually the story of Jesus started to make sense to José Antonio, and he became a Christian believer. What he could not have dreamed was that he would eventually discern a call to the ministry and, after seminary training, become a pastor and preacher. I do not know how the gospel crossed seas to reach Mrs. Pinto in distant Bolivia, the heart of South America, but I am thrilled by the fact that when this simple Bolivian migrant housewife crossed the sea to go to Germany she became a missionary.

Christian mission in the twenty-first century has become the responsibility of a global church. As the missionary facts of our time make us pause in wonder, I begin with doxology by giving thanks to God for the mystery and glory of his gospel. Jesus Christ, God's Son incarnate, is the core of the gospel, which as a potent seed has given birth to innumerable plants. We can locate Jesus in a particular culture at a particular moment in history, for "the Word became flesh and lived among us" (Jn 1:14 NRSV). He lived and taught in Palestine during the first century of our era. After that the story of Jesus has moved from culture to culture, from nation to nation, from people to people. And something strange and paradoxical has taken place: though he was once an obscure peasant from Palestine, Jesus has since been welcomed and adored throughout the world, and people in all cultures and languages have come to see the glory of God in the face of Jesus Christ. Moreover, men and women everywhere feel that he is "theirs," and artists from the past and present have proved the point by representing Jesus in their own cultural terms. At this point in history the global church stands closer than ever to that vision of the seer in Revelation: "A great multitude that no one could count, from every nation, tribe, people and language, standing before the throne and in front of the Lamb" (Rev 7:9).

I cannot but wonder in amazement at the fact that the message of Jesus Christ is "translatable." This means that the gospel dignifies every culture as a valid vehicle for God's revelation. Conversely, this also relativizes every culture: no "sacred" culture or language is the exclusive vehicle that God might use, not even the Hebrew or Aramaic that Jesus spoke, because the Gospels we possess are already a translation from Hebrew or Aramaic into the Greek that was the *koinē*, the lingua franca, of the first century. It is clear that the God who called Abraham to form a nation, and who revealed himself finally in Jesus Christ, intended his revelation to reach all humankind. Jesus stated this clearly in the Great Commission when he instructed the apostles to make disciples of all nations (Mt 28:19); Paul too expressed it in statements such as "God our

Savior . . . wants all men to be saved and to come to a knowledge of the truth" (1 Tim 2:3-4). Through twenty centuries in which diverse empires have risen and fallen, the Holy Spirit has continually driven Christians to obedience, so that today we have a global church.

In this book I shall explore how the church propagates the Christian faith. The heart of "mission" is the drive to share the good news with all, to cross every border with the gospel.

As a community of believers in Jesus Christ, the church performs various functions. It bears *testimony* just by being the church, the company of believers have *fellowship* and feel a sense of belonging, they express joyful gratitude to God in *worship,* they receive *teaching* on the Christian life, they provide *service* in meeting the needs of people both within and outside the church, and they are *prophetic* in the denunciation of evil when God's kingdom is proclaimed. All of these activities are part of the answer to questions such as "What is the church's mission in the world?" or "What does the church exist for?" Sharing the good news, going to "the other" with the message of Jesus Christ, inviting others to Jesus' great banquet, gives a focus and direction to all the other functions. Thus one can say that the church exists for mission and that a church that is only inward looking is not truly the church.

A GLOBAL CHURCH

Over four decades my family and I have had the privilege of being involved in missionary work. The missionary who baptized me in my homeland of Peru at the time I became a university student taught us Christian young people to get involved in planting new churches and evangelizing door to door. From Ruth Siemens, a tentmaker who came to teach in Lima, I got the vision of the university as a mission field. Since 1959 my wife, Lilly, and I have been involved in discipling university students in several Latin American countries, Canada and Spain with the International Fellowship of Evangelical Students. Students were taught to live their life on campuses with a missionary stance, with a sense that

their presence had a purpose in God's plan for the world. After gradua-
tion some of those disciples became missionaries in their own country
or in other parts of the world, and we had the privilege of encouraging
the growing involvement of Latin Americans in global missionary practice and reflection. God has allowed us to experience firsthand the reality
of a global church.

At the start of the twenty-first century, facilities for travel and the flow
of information at a global level through the media, as well as colossal migration movements caused by economic change, allow Christians and
churches everywhere to experience rich and diverse expressions of the
Christian faith. I have met wandering prophets of independent African
churches, native storytellers from Latin American Pentecostal movements, tireless missionary entrepreneurs spreading through the world
from their Korean homeland and Orthodox priests regaining political
weight in the lands that used to be part of the Soviet Empire. Their images fill the pages of our missionary books and the screens of our TVs.
They are also a living testimony to the remarkable variety of human cultures and the uniqueness of the gospel of Jesus Christ.

Migration patterns and refugee movements have helped to bring a
multiplicity of cultures, as well as the different forms that the Christian
church has taken among them, to Europe, the United States and Canada.
At the heart of European and North American cities, Third World cultures, as well as varied expressions of the global church, have taken root.
From the missionary perspective, indigenous churches from faraway
places have become sister churches down the street. By the same token,
growing Muslim or Hindu communities in Western cities have become
a new evangelistic challenge that tests the quality of our Christian lives
as well as our ability to communicate the gospel.

This has consequences for Christians in Western nations, because the
form of Christianity that has developed in the Southern Hemisphere and
has reached the great Western cities is a "popular" form of both Catholicism and Protestantism that we might well call "grass-roots Christian-

ity." It is marked by a culture of poverty, an oral liturgy, narrative preaching, uninhibited emotionalism, maximum participation in prayer and worship, dreams and visions, faith healing, and an intense search for community and belonging. Evangelical leaders who have long emphasized the clear and correct intellectual expression of biblical truth and the rationality of the Christian faith especially need to be sensitive to this new expression of Christianity.

THE SHIFT OF CHRISTIANITY TO THE SOUTH

A systematic observation of the reality of the global church has also made us aware of the new balance of numerical and spiritual strength in the Christian world.[1] As we look at the religious map of the world today we find a marked contrast between the situation at the beginning of the twentieth century and the situation in the early twenty-first century. Scottish missiologist Andrew Walls has described a "massive southward shift of the center of gravity of the Christian world." He understands the history of the Christian church and its mission as a sequence of phases, each of which represents the embodiment of Christianity in a major cultural area. This is followed by the movement forward through transcultural mission in such a way that when that major culture declines, Christianity continues to flourish, now in a different setting. In our times, Walls reminds us,

> The recession of Christianity among the European peoples appears to be continuing. And yet we seem to stand at the threshold of a new age of Christianity, one in which its main base will be in the Southern continents, and where its dominant expressions will be filtered through the culture of those countries. Once again, Christianity has been saved for the world by its diffusion across cultural lines.[2]

The new situation has been hailed by Swiss missiologist Walbert Bühlman, who was a missionary in Africa, as "the coming of the Third Church." He points to the fact that the first thousand years of church history were under the aegis of the Eastern Church, also known as the Orthodox Church, in the Eastern half of the Roman Empire. Then during the second millennium the leading church was the Western Church in the other half of what used to be the Roman Empire. Those familiar with the history of theology also perceive to what degree theological themes, language and categories have reflected this historical situation. Bühlman goes on to say, "Now the Third Millennium will evidently stand under the leadership of the Third Church, the Southern Church. I am convinced that the most important drives and inspirations for the whole church in the future will come from the Third Church."[3]

From my own experience and observation I can point to some examples of the drive and inspiration that come from this Third Church. In 1990 Samuel Cueva and his family were sent from their evangelical church in the central highlands of Peru as Christian missionaries to Spain. When I saw them in Barcelona, they were living in a large block of flats in which Samuel worked as a janitor in order to make ends meet. He believed that evangelical churches in Spain could be the source of new missionary efforts not only to Latin America but also to the Arab world. As he shared about his work, in his eyes was the same fire and enthusiasm for the gospel that I had come to admire in his father, Juan Cueva. Don Juan was a Peruvian businessman who traveled extensively selling medical equipment in the interior of Peru. He also used these sales trips as evangelistic and church-planting occasions. Samuel could have been a successful businessman like other members of his family, but his passion for Christ turned him into an entrepreneurial mission promoter.

During the twentieth century the word *missionary* in Peru was reserved for blond-haired, blue-eyed British or American Christians who had crossed the sea to bring the gospel to the mysterious land of the Incas. Today there is a growing number of Peruvian *mestizos*—dark-eyed, brown-skinned, mixed-race Latin Americans—sent as missionaries to the vast highlands and jungles of Peru as well as to Europe, Africa and

Asia. The single-minded passion for Christ is still the driving force behind mission, but over the course of a century the composition of the missionary force has changed significantly, and changes are also coming to attitudes, methods and, of course, patterns of support for mission.

For several years I had the privilege of being a member of the board of the Overseas Ministries Study Center in New Haven, Connecticut. It had been designed as a place for rest and recreation for missionaries when they returned to their country from the mission field. During the last decades of the twentieth century this organization had to adapt its programs and policies, because the missionaries coming for rest or for continuing education are now Koreans who do medical work in Nigeria or plant churches in the Amazonian jungle, Japanese who work in theological education in Indonesia, or Filipinos who foster economic development in Bangladesh.

At the tables during events in this center you can hear conversations that reflect enthusiasm for what God is doing around the world; there is also a sense that these people feel deeply yet humbly privileged to play a part in the unfolding drama of God's salvific action. The script is still encoded in the vocabulary of Matthew the Evangelist or Paul the apostle, but there are new actors in the drama. Side by side with the Americans or Europeans you now find Asians, Africans and Latin Americans, with their peculiar character traits and eating habits! Like Samuel, my Peruvian friend, these new missionaries have dedicated their life to full-time service with a Christian missionary organization moving across cultural and linguistic borders.

Another missionary force is also at work today, though it does not appear in the records of missionary activity or the databanks of specialists. It is the transcultural witnessing for Christ that takes place as people move around as migrants or refugees, just as in New Testament days. Think, for instance, of the thousands of Filipina women who work as maids in the rich, oil-producing countries where Islam is the official religion and where no European or North American missionaries are allowed. I have had a chance to converse with some of them as, in the midst of daily chores, they sing Christian songs and tell Bible stories to the children they baby-sit. As in biblical times, these women see themselves as witnesses for Christ in a foreign land. They are missionaries "from below" who do not have the power, the prestige or the money from a developed nation, and are not part of a missionary organization. They are vulnerable in many ways but have learned the art of survival, supported by their faith in Jesus Christ and by the assurance that God is with them and will use them in spite of the adverse circumstances in which they have to earn their living.

It is not the case that human and material resources for mission have evaporated in Europe and North America. But, although the missionary enterprise is still strong, especially in North America, many of the older, more traditional missionary organizations do not find as in the past a regular flow of volunteers willing to be trained and sent as missionaries. On the other hand, youth movements such as Youth With a Mission, Operation Mobilization and the Mennonite Central Committee are able to mobilize young volunteers for short-term assignments, with some of these young people later becoming long-term missionaries with other agencies. Every three years in the United States almost twenty thousand university students, eager to learn and to receive an intense and serious missionary challenge, attend the Urbana Student Mission Convention over four days. However, despite the present shift of Christianity to the South, in coming decades Christian mission to all parts of the globe will require resources from both the North and the South to be successful. Pakistani missiologist Michael Nazir-Ali has expressed it well in the title and content of his book *From Everywhere to Everywhere* (Collins, 1990) in which he offers "a world view of Christian mission." It is increasingly evident that responsible, mission-minded Christians today must work together in order to turn into reality the proposal of the Lausanne Covenant: "Missionaries should flow ever more freely from and to all six continents in a spirit of humble service" (par. 9).

MISSION FROM BELOW

Drive and inspiration to move forward and take the gospel of Jesus Christ to the ends of the earth, crossing all kinds of geographical and cultural barriers, is the work of the Holy Spirit. There is an element of mystery when the dynamism of mission does not come from people in positions of power or privilege, or from the expansive dynamism of a superior civilization, but from below—from the little ones, those who have few material, financial or technical resources but who are open to the prompting of the Spirit. Many Western missionary organizations started in the nineteenth and twentieth centuries as humble and insignificant efforts of visionary people before they grew to become large, well-financed organizations. It is not merely coincidence that the form of Christianity that has blossomed in recent decades, especially among the poor urban masses, is that which emphasizes the presence and power of the Holy Spirit: the Pentecostal movement that started among poor, marginalized people. In the words of one of its historians, Pentecostalism is the "vision of the disinherited."[4]

It was in 1927 that Roland Allen (1869-1947) first coined the expression "the spontaneous expansion of the church,"[5] and we can now measure the incredible extent to which a Christian testimony among the masses of this planet has been the result of such spontaneous expansion, especially in China, Africa and Latin America. In many cases such expansion became possible only when indigenous Christians were released from the stifling control of Western missionary agencies.

Another aspect of this new scenario is that while many non-Western cultures are highly receptive to the gospel of Jesus Christ, paradoxically it is within the Western world that we find less receptivity to it. Lesslie Newbigin, a missionary in India for thirty years who then returned to minister among working-class people in Britain, wrote that "the most widespread, powerful and persuasive among contemporary cultures, . . . modern Western culture . . . more than almost any other is proving resistant to the Gospel."[6] Patterns of church growth prove the validity of this observation in the case of North America and Europe today. Several of the old mainline denominations show decline and fatigue with significant numerical losses. Are we here confronted not only with the resistance of Western culture but also with the impotence of the Western churches, crippled by a loss of confidence in the validity of the gospel or by a loss of creativity to change the forms of church life as cultural changes require? Even in European cities I know where the gospel is preached in a relevant way, where people form a welcoming community and where structures such as house churches are created to respond to the urban challenge, the church is still flourishing. In many cases churches of ethnic minorities within declining denominations are also growing vigorously. This constitutes a tough new challenge to partnership in mission.

Precisely at the point at which the influence of Christianity declines in the West, the new global order has brought the so-called Third World into the heart of North America and Europe. Within that environment Christians from old and new churches are called to new partnerships to participate in mission on their own doorstep as well as in global mission. For the old, traditional denominations, partnership with the new immigrant churches brings the need for serious self-appraisal. This is not easy for respectable, middle-class evangelical churches that have a steadier, institutionalized, well-mannered, predictable kind of church. "Mission at our doorstep" may well become the new training ground for the new partnerships that will also carry on mission around the world.

CHANGES IN THE PRACTICE AND THEORY OF MISSION
In the twenty-first century, Christian mission has become truly international, and in order to understand this phenomenon we need a paradigm change in our way of studying it that corresponds to the change in the way mission is now taking place. Indians, Brazilians, Koreans or Filipinos engaging in mission today bring a new set of questions about Christian mission, the way it will be supported, the lifestyle of the missionaries, the

methods they will use, the mission fields to which they will go.

Awareness of the urgency of questions about missionary presence and style has motivated some of the most creative missiological thinking of recent decades. For those whose missiological reflection starts with commitment to the authority of God's Word, the contemporary missionary situation demands an understanding of the Bible that takes into account its cultural setting. The new global dimension of Christianity has brought a new sensitivity to the fact that the text of Scripture can be understood adequately only within its own context, and that the understanding and application of its eternal message demands awareness of our own cultural context. A change of mind and attitude is required, as South African missiologist David Bosch says: "Our point of departure should not be the contemporary enterprise we seek to justify, but the biblical sense of what being sent into the world signifies."[7]

Within the reality of a new global church, a fresh reading of Scripture is possible through the shared work of Christians from different parts of the world. The new perspective requires a firm commitment to the missionary imperatives that are both part of the very structure of our faith and, at the same time, a serious work of biblical scholarship and interpretation. At its best that is what missiology should be.

A MISSIOLOGICAL APPROACH

This book is intended to be a missiological reflection. I define *missiology* as an interdisciplinary approach to understanding missionary action. Missiology examines missionary facts from the perspectives of the biblical sciences, theology, history and the social sciences. It aims to be systematic and critical, but it starts from a positive stance toward the legitimacy of the Christian missionary task as part of the fundamental reason for the being of the church. A missiological approach gives the observer a comprehensive frame of reference in order to look at reality in a critical way. Missiology is a critical reflection of Christians engaged in missionary practice in the light of God's Word.

In that regard one could say that a significant portion of the writings of the apostle Paul are missiological in nature. Think for instance of 2 Corinthians and the way in which Paul refers to his own missionary practice using as points of reference Old Testament teachings as well as the living revelation of God in Jesus Christ through the Spirit. The Spirit-inspired missionary acts of Jesus, Paul and the apostles, as well as their Spirit-inspired reflection on their practice, are authoritative for us, in a way in which no other post-apostolic missionary practice or reflection is authoritative. Biblical scholarship and theology are therefore foundational points of reference for missiological work.

History is also indispensable, and one must recognize immediately that "history" is more than personal journals or collected prayer letters from missionaries. If the facts of mission are going to be established with clarity and truth, the critical work of the professional historian who evaluates and compares sources and interprets them critically becomes necessary. Missionaries in the past tried to follow the drive of the Spirit in obedience to God's Word within their own cultural context. In that way they created "models of missionary obedience" that give us valuable hints for our own missionary obedience today and tomorrow.[8]

In recent years we have also benefited from the systematic and critical observation of mission facts from the perspective of the social sciences. Valuable work in this field has been done, especially by American and Canadian anthropologists with missionary experience such as Eugene Nida, Jacob Loewen, Charles Taber, Paul Hiebert and Miriam Adeney, who have used their scholarly approach to evaluate missionary work and to suggest new methodological lines.[9] Even work from social scientists who are hostile to mission can be helpful for our own self-criticism. History and the social sciences are useful tools for a better understanding of God's Word and of contemporary missionary action, but only that Word is inspired and always fertile to renew the church in mission.

TOWARD AN EVANGELICAL MISSIOLOGY

During the last quarter of the twentieth century, evangelical missiologists embarked on a concerted effort to reflect on the massive accumulated experience of evangelical missionary activity. The Lausanne movement, which has developed since 1974, has been the platform for much of this reflection. Honest evaluation of missionary activity in the light of God's Word, theological truth and new missionary challenges becomes an effort to envision new models of missionary obedience. The widening and deepening of the missiological agenda is now required by the developments in the church and in the world. A minimal degree of historical awareness is indispensable to understand missionary developments.

In the twentieth century there were two cycles of Protestant mission. One had roots in the nineteenth century and kept its strength up to World War II. It represented the official missionary work of the mainline Protestant denominations both in the practice of mission and in the theologizing about it. That period was marked by significant activity from European as well as North American churches, and by theological debate about the nature of the Christian mission and the identity of the young churches growing in Africa, Asia and Latin America. Missiological thinking in this period was carried on within the context of Protestant organizations, especially the International Missionary Council. To this body were related some of the giants of missiological activism and reflection in this period, such as Robert Speer, John R. Mott, Hendrik Kraemer, John A. Mackay and Lesslie Newbigin.

Alongside denominational mission boards is the tradition of "faith missions," which are independent from denominational control and supported by voluntary giving from members of all kinds of Protestant churches. The China Inland Mission (CIM) founded in Great Britain by Hudson Taylor in 1865 was committed to evangelizing where the oldest missions were not going; it had a more flexible methodology and conservative theological views. Known today as the Overseas Missionary Fellowship, this faith mission had great evangelistic zeal and powerfully influenced the concept and practice of other evangelical faith missions in the twentieth century. Often these groups had little regard for theological or missiological reflection, especially when liberal theology became influential in mainline Protestantism.

One of the consequences of World War II was that the United States became a dominant world power. After the war there was a decline in traditional Protestant activity, and a significant expansion of activity and influence from conservative Protestant agencies, especially from the United States. There was also explosive growth of old and new faith missions and parachurch agencies from Europe and North America. At that time evangelical activism expressed itself in organizations with a global reach, such as the International Fellowship of Evangelical Students (IFES), founded in 1947, and the World Evangelical Fellowship, founded in 1956. New specialized agencies for Bible translation, transportation of missionaries, broadcasting media, health services or mass evangelism developed in the United States, and their missionary concepts and methodologies, which reflected American cultural values and mores, became influential around the world. Another trend after the war was the growing impact of the ministry of Billy Graham in North America and Europe, which revealed that those regions had to be considered also as mission fields in which millions of people had lost any significant contact with established churches.

Though Graham insisted that he was an evangelist and not a theologian, he realized that theology was important, and in 1956 he launched *Christianity Today,* a bimonthly periodical that blended evangelistic and missionary fervor with serious theological reflection in an effort to link the evangelistic thrust of Billy Graham with the scholarly work of leading evangelical theologians. The revival of evangelical scholarship in the English-speaking world, after the controversies of fundamentalism, came from the vigorous evangelical student movements that had formed IFES. This was not purely academic scholarship; it had a missionary thrust thanks to the connection with the missionary life of those movements. Through extensive use of Christian media, theological institutions and missionary conferences, these evangelical trends became influential not only in countries receiving missionaries but also in the old sending countries of Europe and North America. These trends give us an insight into the long-term impact of the "Lausanne movement" launched after the International Congress on World Evangelization held in the Swiss city of Lausanne in 1974.

An important antecedent of Lausanne was the Berlin World Congress on Evangelism, sponsored in 1966 by Billy Graham in order to commemorate ten years of *Christianity Today*. In Berlin, John Stott opened a key dimension of the biblical agenda, "mission in Christ's way."[10] In his Bible expositions dealing with the Great Commission in the four Gospels, he shifted the attention from the classic passage of Matthew 28:18-20 to the almost forgotten text of the Commission in John 20:21, "As the Father has sent me, I am sending you." Here we have not only a mandate for mission but also a model of mission style in obedience to the loving design of the Father, patterned by the example of Jesus Christ and driven by the power of the Holy Spirit. At the cross, Jesus Christ died for our salvation and also left a pattern for our missionary life. Mission requires *orthodoxy*, a concern for the integrity of the gospel, but it also requires *orthopraxis*, a concern for the way in which the missionary practice is carried on. Before searching for methods and tools for the communication of a verbal message, we must search for a new style of missionary presence relevant to this moment of human history. When we view the Great Commission within the context of the whole gospel, the Jesus model acquires features that force us to revise our present models.[11]

Reflection after Berlin and toward Lausanne gave many people of my generation around the world a growing conviction that evangelical activism was in danger of carrying on mission as a purely human enterprise. Some schools of church growth, for instance, regarded mission as a manageable task that could be completed by a certain date, using appropriate technology and following business principles of management by objectives. It was necessary to go back to the biblical vision that conceives mission as God's initiative coming from God's love for his creation and from his design in choosing some instruments to use for the salvation and blessing of all of humankind. When in the light of biblical imperatives we revised some of the traditional ways of doing mission, we realized to what degree that pattern had become just a human enterprise and was in danger of being merely the religious side of the expansion of one culture and one empire.

Essentially the shift to the emphasis of John's version of the Commission on *the way* in which Jesus himself accomplished his mission means the abandonment of the imperial mission mentality. Imperial missiology carried on missionary work from a position of superiority: political, military, financial, technological. While "the cross and the sword" symbolized it at the height of Iberian mission in the sixteenth century, "commerce and Christianity" symbolized it at the height of Protestant European mission in the nineteenth century. And in our lifetime "information technology and gospel" has come to symbolize it. In the imperial missiology paradigm, Christianity is thus dependent on the prop and tutelage of another powerful partner.

The paradigm shift that this understanding requires is still underway, especially among the evangelical missionary establishment. Church planting and evangelization in critical areas such as Islamic countries, eastern Europe or central Asia will require a true internationalization of mission, for which a change of mind is necessary. The radical change to which God's Word keeps calling us is a change of mindset and attitude. Without that, the mere accumulation of human and technical resources and the adoption of sophisticated methodologies will not work.

Some missionary leaders among the organizers of the Berlin and Lausanne congresses had thought that these events were going to be golden opportunities to teach churches around the world the missionary and evangelistic methodologies that had been developed in North America.

However, it became evident that evangelicals around the world wanted to affirm a commitment to carry on the task of evangelism and mission with a sense of urgency but also with critical reflection coming from a serious assessment of their context. In my own paper at Lausanne I offered a brief summary of how many speakers in the congresses that followed Berlin had asked key questions about the mission of the church and about the very nature of the gospel.[12]

Several of the contributions from Third World evangelicals at Lausanne articulated that critical reflection about the evangelical missionary activism after World War II. These were not merely academic questions: they arose from the missionary practice of these Christians. It was a reflection that started in an attitude of worship to God, giving thanks for missionary advance in spite of great imperfections, and a commitment to obey his missionary mandate. However, it was also a reflection that tackled some difficult questions such as the need to recover a biblical, holistic concept of Christian mission and to differentiate the gospel of Jesus Christ from the American way of life.[13]

Missiological developments after the Lausanne congress were in many instances an evangelical international and multicultural effort to carry on missiological reflection. This book about Christian mission is written from an evangelical perspective that aims to incorporate the insights gained from a new reading of Scripture, as part of a global evangelical dialogue that takes seriously the facts of the contemporary missionary situation. It is offered in the spirit of the Lausanne Covenant, which states, "We are deeply stirred by what God is doing in our day, moved to penitence by our failures and challenged by the unfinished task of evangelization. We believe the Gospel is God's good news for the whole world and we are determined by his grace to obey Christ's commission to proclaim it to all humankind and to make disciples of every nation" (Lausanne Covenant, Introduction).

2

Mud and Glory

CHRISTIAN MISSION TODAY IS A VAST HUMAN ENTERPRISE in which millions of people are engaged. According to one of the specialist recorders of missionary activity, 420,000 Christian missionaries are involved in transcultural mission around the world today, and the income of global foreign mission amounts to 12 billion U.S. dollars.[1] Such a vast enterprise lends itself to intense research from historians, social scientists and political strategists. A mountain of literature exists on the subject, from sociological explanations about why the urban poor become believers in Christ to studies on how Christians can "market" the church better. There is thus a human side to Christian mission that lends itself to quantification, analysis and explanation.

On the other hand, Christian missionaries themselves frequently emphasize that mission is a divine enterprise and that their engagement cannot be explained or understood by purely human factors. They see themselves engaged in mission as a faith commitment, a response to what God has revealed about himself and what he has done for them, a commitment consistent with Christian truth. The great pioneer of transcultural Christian mission, and probably the person who has most influenced its subsequent development over the centuries, is the apostle Paul. In

2 Corinthians, where he deals most extensively with Christian mission, Paul uses a metaphor that conveys the tension and paradox of the human and the divine in Christian mission. He writes about the glorious power of God manifested in the creation of this world and how that same power is in action whenever a person comes to faith and is given "the light of the knowledge of the glory of God in the face of Christ" (2 Cor 4:6). Then he proceeds to describe the human condition of the messengers of this glorious gospel: "But we have this treasure in jars of clay to show that this all-surpassing power is from God and not from us" (2 Cor 4:7).

"Jars of clay" is an image that takes us back to the biblical teaching about the human condition, the terrestrial nature, the fragility and the powerlessness of missionaries, in contrast to the glorious power of God. Paul elaborates on this point by describing the conditions under which he himself and his missionary colleagues worked in those early days of mission history. His words communicate well the living paradoxes missionaries were: "We are hard pressed on every side, but not crushed; perplexed, but not in despair; persecuted, but not abandoned; struck down, but not destroyed" (2 Cor 4:8-9). The thrust of this section of Paul's letter is to stress God's initiative in Christian mission in contrast to the human tendency toward pride and the cult of personality that was creeping into the attitude of the Corinthian Christians. This Pauline emphasis on God's initiative in mission must be recovered now precisely because in our time, outside observers such as critical historians, social scientists and even fiction writers have subjected missionary activity to the scrutiny of their critical tools of analysis. Moreover, in the midst of their busyness, and frequently without intending it, missionaries and mission leaders themselves tend to forget that "mission is God's mission," not just a great human enterprise. We can become deluded idealists if we forget the human dimension of mission, but we lose perspective and a sense of direction when we forget the divine dimension of mission. A sound grasp of the history of missions helps us to avoid becoming idealistic or paralyzed by cynicism.

HOW DO YOU TELL THE STORY?

In this chapter I limit myself to a brief outline of the history of missions. When you tell a story you always have *a point of view* that influences your selection of the parts of the story you decide to include, the characters you choose to mention and the facts you take as milestones or decisive points. In the telling of the story of missions during the latter part of the twentieth century there have been efforts to correct the Eurocentric perspective predominant in the academic world in the West. This perspective majored on the development of ecclesiastical structures and institutions, taking what existed in Europe and the United States as the norm. Mission came to be seen as the effort to reproduce those structures and institutions in the rest of the world. Contemporary revisionists argue a loss of memory regarding important aspects of the story of missions, especially of the early church. They have tried to recover that memory for the benefit of the new churches and the new generations of missionaries.[2]

I find a valuable example of this in the book *The Memory of the Christian People*, a historical study about the first three centuries of the Christian church from a missiological perspective. Its author, Eduardo Hoornaert, is a Catholic priest who went as a missionary from Belgium to Brazil in 1958 and has remained there. He studied classical philology and ancient history at Louvain and theology at Bruges; most of his mission work has taken place in the poor and explosive region of the Brazilian northeast. Hoornaert was active in the development of what is known as the "popular church," the Christian base communities, and he has especially researched the history of the church among natives and blacks in Brazil. In his writings he is committed to present "the perspective of the poor and the marginalized." His questions come from his missionary practice among the base communities.

At several points in his book Hoornaert establishes parallels between the life of the Christian communities among the poor of Brazil and the life of the early church before Constantine, because, as he says in his preface, "There is actually a surprising parallel between the current experience of the base communities and the life of the first Christian communities. The pastoral ministers of today's base communities who so enthusiastically exclaim, 'Why, this is the way the Christians lived' are far from mistaken."[3] This is also my observation. I have been at church meetings in places as diverse as Harare in Zimbabwe, Manila in the Philippines, the Hispanic section of Philadelphia in the United States and Quechua-speaking churches in the south of Peru. It is amazing how easily people in these churches move from the book of Acts to their own context. The conditions are so similar!

For Hoornaert the reading of history with a new key brings to light some aspects of the missionary life of the early church that have special significance for those who work among the poor and displaced in the margins of society. We rediscover the important role played by laypersons, women, children and the elderly; the place of money and the community of goods; and the social dimension of theological controversies. This kind of reading provides fresh insights into the theology of the New Testament epistles. Hoornaert finds that in 1 Peter and 1 Corinthians the poor and the marginalized are those "chosen" by God for his missionary purposes. This perspective would be in open contrast with the one inaugurated by Eusebius of Caesarea, the fourth-century historian who became an influential model for the way Christians have written church history. Though the value of Eusebius's work is undeniable, Hoornaert believes he had an axe to grind, an ideology that reflected his enthusiastic acceptance of Christianity's privileged position granted by the emperor Constantine, as well as his choice of bishops as the most important characters in the story. The conclusion is that "Eusebius" theology, altogether novel for the time, can only be characterized as an "imperial theology," a theology of empire. As to the choice of characters, "Eusebius founded a new Christian literary genre, one which sees no problem in equating Christian memory with an 'apostolic succession' in the sense of a simple succession of bishops in local churches."[4]

Hoornaert also pays special attention to the role of women in the records of the early church, reminding us that "service to the least ones" was most faithfully practiced by women (Lk 8:1-3; 23:55—24:1). Christian women have continued to care for bodies, to provide food, homes and clothing, "while men have only plunged deeper and deeper into the struggle for power and prestige."[5] Women supplied much of the infrastructure of the first communities: homes for meetings (Acts 12:12-16), lodging for itinerant preachers (Acts 16:12-15) and clothing for widows (Acts 9:36-39); they also shared in the leadership of communities (Acts 18:26-27; Rom 16:6, 12; Phil 4:2-3) and prophesied (Acts 21:9). Careful observation of church life anywhere shows that this role of women has continued up to the present. However, there has been a loss of memory about the participation of women in missions.

This loss of memory in the way of telling the story is due to what American historian Ruth Tucker calls a "male dominated institutionalized church [that] has deeply entrenched concepts of power, authority and office—and women have not fit into the scheme."[6] Tucker wrote her book *Guardians of the Great Commission* precisely because her research into the history of missions showed how deeply involved women were, both overseas and on the home front. However, when she studied the standard English works by well-known authors on the history of missions, women were absent, which reflects an incredible loss of memory, she says, "in light of the magnitude and influence of this female missionary movement."

> This is true of the mission texts written by Stephen Neill and J. Herbert Kane. Neither author even mentions the women's missionary movement . . . yet the women's missionary movement not only sponsored thousands of missionaries and Bible women and built schools and hospitals, but it also produced some of the greatest mission strategists and missiologists of the late nineteenth and early twentieth centuries.[7]

Tucker finds in the women she studies a painful awareness of discrimination, and in some cases women missionaries had long battles for justice and liberation that are well documented. She also deals with women who excelled in missionary writing and became influential through it, such as Elisabeth Elliott, Amy Carmichael and Mildred Cable. One of Tucker's conclusions makes an important point from the perspective of the historian:

> Many of the most insightful and honest books about the realities of missionary work have been written by women. . . . Without the woman's perspective, missionary literature would be sorely deficient. The trials of family life and the inner spiritual struggles are often dealt with in greater depth by women, and women are often more open in admitting their own personal conflicts than men are.[8]

I have found that a reasonable approach to the writing of the history of missions falls between two extremes. The first is the *hagiographical*: chronicles and biographies that present the lives of missionaries and their work, such as the old "books of saints." Heroes and heroines are cast as angels with no reference to their human weaknesses. Some histories of missions are only summaries of autobiographies or promotional material of this type. Generally these stories are not related to the larger picture of national and international history that surrounded the missionary enterprise, and no attention is paid to social, cultural and historical factors. Usually the viewpoint of Christians at the receiving end of missionary work is not taken into account.

The second extreme is the kind of critical approach followed generally by recent *non-Christian authors*. These use sources such as minutes of mission boards or church assemblies, missionary correspondence, journals and diaries, or promotional literature, which may be scrutinized by any interested person. Therefore, the missionary enterprise can be recorded and analyzed by historians or social scientists who, having no Christian conviction, bring a totally different (sometimes quite hostile) outlook to the task of interpreting missionary sources. Such critical approaches to Christian missions have sometimes uncovered realities that hagiography had kept hidden or simply not dealt with.

A third, more mature approach is possible, one where evangelical students of missions come to terms with historical realities and understand the passion and commitment to Christ in the missionaries, as well as their limitations and shortcomings. The hard facts of social, economic and political realities that surround the missionary enterprise have to be considered. From such awareness will develop a more relevant history for the coming generations of missionaries. Luke's history of the initial expansion of the church in the apostolic period, in his Gospel and in the book of Acts, is an excellent piece of historical writing. Though written from within the community of faith, it does not deal with the historical material in a naive way. Luke's clear grasp of the historical and social context, as well as his gripping description of life and relationships, makes it a superb example of mature historical writing.

TWENTY CENTURIES OF MISSIONARY ADVANCE

In the twenty-first century we are privileged to have a unique vantage point from which to look at the past twenty centuries of missionary advance. As historian Kenneth Scott Latourette wrote in 1948, when his seven-volume *History of the Expansion of Christianity* was already completed, "No fact of history is more amazing than the spread of the influence of Jesus." He reminds us that at the time of Jesus' crucifixion there was, humanly speaking, no foreseeable possibility that one day his message would be taken to the ends of the earth. The odds were overwhelmingly stacked against the idea that one day his simple life would so powerfully impact human history! For Latourette there is a pattern in the missionary spread of the gospel in which several factors (mud and glory) intervene. He notes a pattern of ebb and flow:

> From Jesus, through Christianity, have issued impulses which have helped to shape every phase of civilization. His influence has grown with the passing of the years and has never been so powerful as in the past cen-

tury and a quarter [Latourette is writing in 1948]. Its course has been like that of an incoming tide. Like the tide it has moved forward in waves. Each major wave has been followed by a major recession. But each major wave has set a new high-water mark and each major recession has been less pronounced than its predecessor.[9]

This pattern of ebb and flow led Latourette to organize his history of Christian missions into eight stages. The initial advance to A.D. 500 was followed by the first and greatest recession (500-950); the second great age of advance (950-1350) gave way to the second major recession (1350-1500); then followed the third great age of advance (1500-1750) and the third major recession (1750-1815); while the fourth great age of advance (1815-1914) had finished just before Latourette wrote. In a way, the reference to ebb and flow tempers his vision, which is not triumphalistic but comes from a faith perspective matched by his in-depth knowledge of the facts.

The second half of the twentieth century was marked by the emergence of the Third World, the revolt of new independent nations against colonialism from Europe and North America, and the tensions of the Cold War. However, the period between 1945 and 1989 can be described as a time of missionary activism. By 1970, American missiologist Ralph Winter, an enthusiastic follower of Latourette, described the twenty-five years after 1945 as "unbelievable."[10] His optimism was based on statistics of missionary activity and popular studies of numerical church growth that were becoming influential, especially among missionaries and people on evangelical mission boards.

If we take into account the secularization of Europe and the paganization of North America, or the lack of depth in some of the younger churches, it is debatable whether in the initial years of the twenty-first century we are in a period of advance or recession. Analysis of existing figures takes us to a sobering conclusion: "The overall percentage of those who say they are Christians in the world today is about the same as in 1900—34%."[11] We cannot overlook the amazing growth of the church in Africa, parts of Asia, and Latin America, as well as the new vitality in eastern Europe. However, Latourette's analysis of the previous nineteen centuries provides clues for a more realistic and sober perspective, and discernment with which to evaluate mere numerical growth.

Andrew Walls agrees with Latourette that "the history of Christianity has not been one of steady progress, let alone of resistless triumph." In other words, he says, "The Christian story is serial; its center moves from place to place. No one church or place or culture owns it. At different times different peoples and places have become its heartlands, its chief representatives. Then the baton passes on to others."[12] Walls organizes his overview of the history of missions into six ages. The interpretative key he uses is the relationship between the life of the church, culture and mission. He sees two principles in action: the "indigenizing" principle, by which the Christian faith takes root in a particular culture to the point of sometimes becoming one with it but losing some of its distinctive elements; and the "pilgrim" principle, by which a missionary impulse takes the faith to other cultures and in a way preserves the faith through missionary action. In the outline I offer here, I use principles from Latourette and Walls, adding some observations about the relation between "mission and empire," which became especially significant as the twentieth century closed.

A JEWISH CHURCH IN MISSION

The initial followers of Jesus Christ were Jews. If we forget that fact we do not understand much of the New Testament. The church at Jerusalem after Pentecost was basically a Jewish church, one of the many sects within Judaism. The daily life of these disciples followed the predominant Jewish cultural patterns, and when they first organized themselves to communicate the gospel they were a band of itinerant prophets, healers and teachers. Jesus' missionary instructions to his first envoys, as recorded by Matthew (10:5-15) and Luke (9:1-6; 10:1-12), make sense only within the traditions of the Jewish nation.

However, these disciples were a particular kind of Jewish people. There is a sentence pregnant with meaning in the lips of the old man Simeon when he meets the child Jesus, taking him in his arms and praising God:

> My eyes have seen your salvation,
>> which you have prepared in the sight of all people,
> a light for revelation to the Gentiles
>> and for glory to your people Israel. (Lk 2:30-32)

Simeon's words summarize well the hope of Israel within a missionary vision that had a well-preserved memory of the purpose of God in forming that nation. Those who received and followed Jesus were people such as Simeon, the old Anna, Mary, Elizabeth, Zechariah, the Twelve and Stephen, whom Luke describes as devout, righteous and filled with the Holy Spirit—Jews with a sense of mission who acknowledged Jesus as the Messiah, God's missionary to Israel and to the world.

As we consider the "Jewishness" of that initial moment we should not forget that God had been at work in the world preparing it for the coming of Christ and for the missionary spreading of his gospel. In many cases, synagogues of the Jewish Diaspora, spread all over the Roman Empire, were to become the initial base for the evangelization of Gentiles. We find in the book of Acts many proselytes of Judaism, such as Cornelius and Lydia, who had been attracted to the message of the Old Testament and the lifestyle of Israel and who then became disciples of Jesus. And we also find that the Septuagint, the Jewish Bible translated into the Greek language, became a precious instrument for the first Christian missionaries as they articulated and spread their faith.

Among the missionaries of this first generation were those as different as Peter and Paul. Both were faithful and pious Jews, but they were worlds apart culturally, and this accounts for their distinctive calls and styles—one, an uneducated, plain, Galilean fisherman for whom eating with non-Jewish people was anathema; the other, an urbane, educated rabbi born in the cosmopolitan city of Tarsus (a crossroads of trade and culture) who valued the privilege of his Roman citizenship. What they had in common was that at a given moment in their life they heard the call of Christ sending them on a mission, and they became obedient apostles. The samples of their sermons in the book of Acts, as well as their writing in the epistles that carry their names as authors, are marked by a deep commitment to Jesus Christ as Savior and Lord, which is central to their way of understanding and expounding the truth of the gospel. Both of them, though in different ways, dealt with the consequences of the fact of Christ for their own perception of their Jewish faith. Paul was more explicit about his missionary methods and the financial support of his ministry. With him we clearly move into the next stage of missions history.

MISSIONARY EXPANSION INTO THE GRECO-ROMAN WORLD

There is another aspect of the New Testament we can perceive only if we examine it with the questions that come from missionary action. The different personal stories, the development of teaching and doctrine, the conflicts among disciples, and the missionary methods may be understood only by keeping in mind that at this stage, the gospel moves from one culture to another, from the Jewish world into the world shaped by Roman imperial dominion and Greek culture. This is the beginning of the second stage of missions history, a formative period where the human and the divine interact in the development of patterns that will shape the life of Christian churches down to the present.

In Paul's narrative of his own call to mission, he remembers specifically that he heard a voice speaking his own Hebrew language (Acts 26:14). However, the voice told him that he was being sent to proclaim the gospel to the Gentiles, the non-Hebrews (Acts 26:17). The significance of that specific call is a subject to which Paul returns frequently in his writings, because some Jewish believers in Christ did not understand Paul's call to evangelize Gentiles as part of what God was doing in the world to accomplish his saving purpose.

During the initial advance of the gospel, the Roman Empire was the historical and cultural background, but the missionaries provided the action. The background is necessary but is not the determinant factor for missionary action. Some New Testament scholars would argue that both Paul and Luke had a positive attitude toward the Roman Empire and that the intention and style of Luke-Acts as well as the teaching of Romans 13 show this attitude. Henry Cadbury quotes these words from a classicist: "It is not often stated, yet perhaps it is the fact, that the best short general picture of the *pax Romana* and all that it meant—good roads and posting, good police, freedom from brigandage and piracy, freedom of movement, toleration and justice is to be found in the experiences written in Greek, of a Jew who happened to be a Roman citizen—that is, in the Acts of the Apostles."[13] However, it is clear from the historical narrative in Acts and the text of the epistles that in no case whatsoever does Paul appear to the participant in the story, or to the modern reader, as an agent of the Roman Empire; he is an ambassador of Jesus Christ.

In this initial stage the missionary advance of the church against all odds was incredible. To the modern observer, aware of twenty centuries of missions history, the growth of the early church in the first century continues to be an enigma. It can be viewed as nothing less than a miraculous work of God, who used people wholeheartedly committed to Christ at the risk of martyrdom, sensitive to the direction of the Holy Spirit and ready to use all avenues open for the advance of the gospel. Conversion to Christ brought a Christian experience that included *belief* in the gospel of Christ, who was confessed as Savior and Lord by his atoning death in the cross and resurrection; a change of *behavior* in order to live a life worthy of the gospel, patterned on Jesus' example; and *belonging* to the body of Christ, the new humanity God was creating in his church.

The faith of Jesus Christ had to be lived and interpreted in dialogue with narrow Jewish provincialism, with skeptical and sophisticated Greek philosophizing, with the Roman cult of the supreme principles of law, order and power, and with the deeply attractive spiritual experiences of the mystery religions. It was not only an intellectual task but also a resocializing experience and a spiritual struggle. The prologue to the Fourth Gospel (John 1:1-18) and the discourse of Paul in the Areopagus of Athens (Acts 17:22-31) are examples of the pioneer task for the first generation of transcultural missionaries of coming to terms with the intellectual challenge of Greek thought. Evangelizing the Greek mind predominant in the Roman Empire required that missionaries be competent in the Greek language and intellectually capable of adapting Greek categories and ways of reasoning in order to express the Christian faith.[14] As time went on, new churches were planted and new cities reached, and ensuing generations of leaders such as Irenaeus, Tertullian, Origen and Clement of Alexandria became the apologists who expounded the gospel for the new generations of believers. Their literary work made the Christian faith a valid alternative for young minds in search of wisdom. This intellectual task complemented the testimony of the daily life of simple Christians, and it is important to remember what historian Justo González wrote:

> In the centuries before Constantine, most of the expansion of Christianity took place not due to the work of people dedicated exclusively to that task but thanks to the constant testimony of hundreds and thousands of merchants, slaves and Christians condemned to exile who went on giving testimony for Jesus Christ wherever life would take them, and in that way formed new communities in places where the "professional" missionaries had not yet arrived.[15]

González considers Gregory of Pontus to be typical of missionaries of that period. Gregory and his brother Athenodorus were converted to Christianity while studying under Origen, whose scholarship and intellectual gifts attracted them. He taught them logic, physics, geometry and astronomy, but he challenged them to go further and to consider the "true philosophy": the Christian faith. Gregory had an attractive personality, and he evangelized in the same logically persuasive way in which he himself had been brought to faith. For him Christianity was not just a speculative philosophy but truth that had to accompany virtue. When he moved to the Pontus region he had to be a pastor and teacher of very simple people for whom the faith meant first and foremost a moral change and a new way of life. In this Gregory had also been schooled by his teacher Origen, who, as he recalled, "incited us much more to the practice of virtue, and stimulated us by the deeds he did more than by the doctrines he taught."[16] Origen was one of the apologists who was martyred during the persecution unleashed by the Roman emperor Decius.

Imperial persecution was one of the facts of the first three centuries of missionary advance of the church. Religion was an important factor in the structure of the empire, for it provided cohesion among the population and an ideology that fostered loyalty to the empire and served as a rationale for the actions of the emperor. At some point, however, the emperors began to claim a divine origin and nature. When significant numbers of the population embraced faith in Christ as Lord, the church became an obstacle to imperial designs, and Christians came to be considered public enemies. Imperial persecution was an effort to wipe out Christianity, but in many cases Christians dying as martyrs attracted even more people to the faith.

The situation changed when the emperor Constantine adopted Christianity, ushering in a new era of acceptance and privilege for Christian believers. Constantine issued the Edict of Milan in the year 313, thus inaugurating a period in which the church was officially tolerated within a framework of religious freedom. Later, imperial support for the church intensified to the point that in the year 381 the Edict of Thessalonica established Christianity as the state religion. In the text of this edict is an affirmation that Christianity is true religion. Theologian Gustavo Gutiérrez, who has written a monumental study of the development of the way

Iberian missions evangelized the natives of the Americas by military force, comments:

> This defense of the true religion is asserted to the detriment of religious freedom: anyone rejecting Christianity will be punished by the civil power. Religious unity is reestablished in the empire and by force. Emerging from the condition of mere tolerance Christianity quickly comes to be a "state religion." Thus the ideal of a Christian state is born and it will have enormous influence in the history of the church all the way to today.[17]

From the missiological perspective the long-term consequences were detrimental to the ethos and spirit of mission the way Jesus taught and practiced it. Gutiérrez reminds us that as time went on "a series of means of force would be legitimated not for *imposing* the faith, but—it will be said—simply for *fostering* it. . . . The repression of evil, for example, thanks to the fear it inspires, will further good behavior."[18] This new position of the church explains the development of a theological basis for the use of violent methods, thus justifying not only the forced conversion of Muslims and Jews in the Middle Ages but also the use of persecution, torture and execution to combat what the established church considered heresy. After the imperial blessing on the church there was a massive wave of conversions that were either superficial or plainly spurious.

The new situation also meant that the imperial policies of Christian emperors now influenced the definition of dogmas. Tensions between the East and the West within the Roman Empire were the background of theological controversies after the fourth century. We do not know much, for instance, about the vigorous missionary movement that the Nestorians of the Eastern Church carried on in Persia and China, because the Western Church, which dominated from Rome, labeled Nestorians heretics and condemned them.

Commerce in the Eastern part of the Roman Empire, following the trade routes, greatly helped the expansion of Christianity. Christian merchants from Syria and Mesopotamia carried their faith to the places where they established trading colonies. For instance, they were the earliest Christian presence in India, many centuries before the Jesuits or William Carey went there. There is today an influential church in India that traces its origins back to those days and has even kept the Syriac language in its liturgy.

THE EVANGELIZATION OF BARBARIANS AND THE MAKING OF EUROPE

If we look at missions in the most recent centuries we see Europe as the center from which the Christian faith moved to the Americas, Asia and Africa. During the second millennium after Christ, the Christian faith was defined and Christian theology articulated in Europe. The great thinkers and artists who left their mark on what today we call Western culture were mostly European. But we must remember that the Christian faith was born outside Europe and that once upon a time Europe itself was evangelized. In fact, Europe was formed during a historical process in which Christian mission played an important part. This earlier history is not as well known today as the missionary process out of Europe in recent centuries. When we look at this process we see a picture of lights and shadows, of mud and glory. Evangelicals in the so-called Third World should not forget that such an ambiguous history is also our own history. And if we are to be missionaries in the years to come we would do well to learn from that process.

The world of the Roman Empire and Greek culture was in a state of fatigue and internal moral decline by the time the emperors embraced the Christian church. The empire was also threatened by invasion of barbarians from the east and the north. Having used Greek culture and Roman institutions for its own purposes, the church became the guardian of the best from that heritage as time went on. At the same time moral decline, combined with floods of nominal Christians entering the church, stimulated a desire for a return to the spiritual and moral qualities of New Testament Christianity. A conviction developed that those qualities could be cultivated only by renouncing the lifestyle predominant in society. This spiritual restlessness and impatience with secular life were the seeds from which the monastic movement grew. The monks, consecrated to a separate life of prayer, contemplation and action, took upon themselves the task of going to proclaim the gospel in distant lands and evangelizing the waves of barbarians then invading the empire. The monasteries became advance posts of Christian mission and deposits of classical culture, and in many instances missionaries had a dual task: they were *civilizers*, communicating the values of classical culture to rough bands of roving invaders, and also *evangelizers*, inviting the invaders to accept the radical message of Jesus Christ.

The barbarians lived a tribal life characterized by a strong sense of ethnic identity and loyalty to their chiefs or kings, which developed within the framework of constant wars of survival or conquest. A pattern of communal acceptance of Christianity appeared, by which if the chief was attracted to the faith and convinced of its value, the whole tribe accompanied him in a collective decision. About Clovis, king of the Franks who was baptized around 496, Latourette remarks, "Although Clovis did not employ force to induce his Frankish followers to conform to his example, his baptism gave a powerful stimulus to that of his nation." He goes on to say, "Again and again in Great Britain the conversion of one of the Anglo-Saxon kingdoms followed upon that of its king. . . . More than one Slavic prince engineered the conversion of his subjects. The conversion of the Bulgars was accomplished largely because of the initiative of their King Boris, and the leadership of his great son Simeon."[19] The historical memory of these European nations is connected with the experience of Christianization in their origins. For Russia, the missionary work of Cyril and Methodius, two monks from Constantinople, was a key element in its formation as a nation. In fact the Russian alphabet is called Cyrillic because it is an adaptation of the Greek alphabet worked out by none other than Cyril and his missionary colleague.

As the Constantinian alliance of church and state developed, the day came when military power was used for the conversion of peoples, because their Christianization was necessary for the political strategy of an emperor. The conversion of the Saxons in what is today Germany is an interesting example. In the year 800, Charlemagne, king of the Franks, became emperor in an effort to revive the western Roman Empire. For him the Christianization of the Saxons was necessary to pacify that region, and indeed since 732 there had been initiatives to send monks for that purpose. These missionaries were part of a military enterprise to subdue the Saxons, after whose defeat prisoners were forced to be baptized following a brief period of instruction. By the year 777, Westphalia was dominated and divided into small mission territories to be evangelized from important monasteries spread along the region. Revolts flared up against the conquerors, and pagan cults were revived as symbols of protest. But by the year 793, Charlemagne forced the most rebellious groups to move far away into exile and thus achieved the complete domination of Saxony.[20]

This mixture of religious and military motives was also at the heart of the crusades, which had a strong impact on the history of Europe. Beginning in the year 622, Islam, a monotheistic faith that had taken elements from Judaism and Christianity, expanded from its original birthplace in the Arabian Peninsula and conquered several strongholds of Eastern Christianity such as Syria and Egypt. By the year 698 the whole north of Africa had been conquered, and by 711 Spain was invaded and the Iberian Peninsula occupied. Muslim advance into Europe could be stopped only at the Battle of Tours. Islam was committed to expanding with a strong missionary, conquering vocation. Vast territories became subject to Muslim control, and, though there was no bloody persecution, Christians were required to pay extra taxes, no church buildings could be built, and conversion to Christianity was forbidden. The avowed purpose of the crusades was to recover the Holy Land from Muslim domination, but there were many political and economic factors that steered them. Modern historians agree that the crusades were one stage in the expansion of northern and western European peoples that would later carry them over the globe. However, it is important to keep in mind that during these centuries, forced conversion and wars attempting to promote Christianity were not the only missionary method. As Latourette observes, "It was not alone factors indifferent or antagonistic to the temper of Jesus and his message which accounted for the spread of Christianity in these parlous centuries. Within Christianity and deriving ultimately from Jesus was a vitality without which the faith would not have persisted or have won fresh converts."[21]

An overview of the history of missions would be incomplete without a reference to the great missionary orders that arose at the time Europe itself was being formed. They continue to be the main instrument for missionary work in the Roman Catholic Church and have influenced the concept of many missionary agencies. Like the universities which also appeared during that period, they attracted energetic young people eager to learn, open to adventure and ready to accept the disciplines of a consecrated life. Bands of young people gathered around scholars to form the guilds out of which developed the oldest colleges and universities in Europe. In a similar way, people gathered around spiritual teachers and formed the great missionary orders, as is the case of the Franciscans and the Dominicans. These orders were characterized by mobility and became the new focus of missionary activity that replaced the monastery, which for five centuries up to that point had been the heart of the missionary enterprise. As Stephen Neill points out, these two orders, like their founders, were very different in style and in the way in which they formulated their specific call. Francis of Assisi wanted to serve the poor and imitate the lifestyle of Jesus, while Domingo de Guzman wanted to consecrate his intellect to the task of preaching and defending the faith. "But in each lived a genuine missionary impulse. Before the thirteenth century is out, we shall find Franciscans at the ends of the known earth. And about the Dominicans formed the *Societas Fratrum peregrinantium propter Christum inter gentes*, 'the company of brethren dwelling in foreign parts among the heathen for the sake of Christ.'"[22] Two centuries later came the Jesuits, in whose ranks were found mainly college and university people who gathered around Ignacio de Loyola (Ignatius of Loyola) and became heavily involved in missionary action in Asia and in the Americas.

In the Franciscan order was Ramon Lull (1235-1315), a Spanish troubadour who converted to Christ and left us mystical writings and a model of missionary practice and reflection. Historian Neill says that "Ramon Lull must rank as one of the greatest missionaries in the history of the Church. Others were filled with an equally ardent desire to preach the gospel to the unbelievers, and if necessary to suffer for it; it was left to Lull to be the first to develop a theory of missions—not merely to wish to preach the gospel, but to work out in careful detail how it was to be done."[23] In Lull's days the people to be evangelized were the Saracens, who were Muslims, and he conceived a missionary methodology that could be summarized in three points: (1) a comprehensive and accurate knowledge of their language, (2) the composition of a book in which the truth of the Christian religion should be demonstrated logically, and (3) a willingness to be a faithful and courageous witness among the Saracens, even at the cost of life itself.[24] This methodology was in open contrast to the warlike mentality of the crusades against the Saracens that characterized the period of history in which he lived.

EMPIRE AND MISSION FROM EXPANDING EUROPE

The Constantinian marriage of church and state evolved, and eventually mission became closely associated with the imperial enterprise of European nations. This alliance reached its apex in the sixteenth century when Portugal and Spain became global empires through exploration and military conquest. Probably there has been no point at which missionary action and imperial action have been so closely linked in theory and practice as in the evangelization of the Americas. The Iberian conquest of the Americas was rightly called by some of its agents "the last of the crusades." Even for men critical of that enterprise there was no question about the right of the pope as head of the church to give his dear children, the kings of Spain and Portugal, the right to evangelize in the world discovered by Columbus. For them, conquering in the name of Spain and thus enlarging the reach of the Spanish Empire was synonymous with enlarging the kingdom of God.

Missionary work from Spain was carried on under the patronage of the Spanish monarchs, an arrangement called *Real Patronato de Indias*. This meant complete control of missionary activity by the interests of the empire. Religion was instrumental in the transfer of a social and economic system from the Iberian Peninsula to the new territories, and theology provided the rationale for it. The document called "Requerimiento" (Summons) was read to the Indians before staging battle against them. It opened with a theological exposition going back to creation, Israel, Jesus Christ and then the apostle Peter and his successor, the pope, who had authorized Spanish monarchs to conquer those territories in order to evangelize them. The natives were thus required to submit and accept the conquerors peacefully or be conquered by force. There was fervent theological debate at the University of Salamanca to decide if the natives of the Americas were truly and wholly human or if, because of their inferiority, the Spanish were entitled to dominate and rule them. In that debate the great defender of the Indians was Bartolomé de Las Casas (1474-1566). This Dominican priest combined his missionary practice in what is today Mexico and Guatemala with his voluminous writings and his academic debates to prove the humanity of the natives and the need for a missionary methodology patterned after the example of Jesus Christ.[25]

Las Casas is representative of missionaries of the different orders who not only were involved in the tasks of evangelizing the natives, establishing new churches and ministering to the conquerors but who also used their education and influence to defend the new Christians from the exploitation and oppression of the Iberian colonial enterprise. A historian from Puerto Rico writes:

The evangelization undertaken by the Dominicans was not aimed at mass baptism: they were more interested in quality than quantity and sought to give those converted a solid grounding in the new faith. The methods of this first community rested on four pillars: understanding of Indian languages and religion, doctrinal teaching in the form of stories rather than theological abstractions, frequent preaching from the scriptures and the witness of the missionary's own poverty and life of prayer.[26]

However, the same historian acknowledges that "the model of peaceful evangelization and inculturation put forward by the Dominicans and other religious orders was defeated by the evangelizing program of the crown which was to convert the Indies into a colonial Christendom."[27] The Jesuits developed the idea of the "reductions" as an effort to create spaces where Indians could live by themselves, far from the exploitation and abuse of the colonial enterprise. They entered into conflict with other orders and with secular clergy who wanted to baptize the Indians quickly in order to use them as slave labor and to tax them with the tithes and offerings that were part of the religious system. This is the background of the famous film *The Mission* and the book on which it is based.[28]

By the nineteenth century, the great century of Protestant missions, there had been important changes. The British Empire was the background for the missionary enterprise, but the alliance of empire and mission was no longer as clear as in the sixteenth century. Protestant missions were generally less linked to government interests than Catholic missions in the sixteenth century, partly because of the modernizing and secularizing influence of Protestantism itself and the slow disestablishment of the churches in Europe. There were more tensions between missionaries and imperialists. When the famous British missionary William Carey (1761-1834) went to India, he was not welcomed by the colonial authorities there and so moved to a territory under Danish control. However, as French theologian and sociologist Roger Mehl has observed, in the case of Africa during the nineteenth century, missionary expansion was contemporaneous with colonial expansion, and the imperial presence of Europe created what he calls "a materially favorable circumstance" for mission:

> The missionary appeared in the wake of the colonialist, merchant, or soldier. He profited from the routes opened by the colonialist, from the zones of security created by him. He borrowed his boats. He established his posts in the proximity of administrative and commercial centers. Thus a *de facto* solidarity was established between colonization and mission. It is necessary to emphasize that this solidarity was not consciously desired by mission. Indeed, there are numerous facts that attest to the existence of conflicts between colonization and mission.[29]

The ambiguity of this relationship between mission and empire is evident as we consider other aspects of missionary work in this period. The missionary movement, especially in the case of Asia and Africa, contributed to the creation of a bourgeoisie that helped in the administration of the empire. Missionary schools played an important role in this process. Also from that educated middle class was to come the leadership of the various nationalist movements whose role was crucial in the fight for independence, especially during the twentieth century in Asia and Africa. In the case of Latin America, the British imperial expansion came at the time when the colonies from Spain were fighting for independence, and Protestant missions was possible due to the space provided by that struggle. James Thomson (1788-1854), pioneer of Protestant missions and Bible work in Latin America, was a friend of the anticolonial leaders, who welcomed his educational work as a contribution to democracy and freedom. Similarly, in the twentieth century, when the United States helped liberate Korea from Japanese colonialism, American missionaries were welcomed and regarded as part of the liberating presence.

Missionary work that originated from the United States held sway during much of the twentieth century. The issue of mission and empire in this case took a new turn because of the unique religious experience of that country. The United States is the first major Western world power in which there has been no established church. Within this situation the presence and life of the churches rely on a great amount of *volunteerism* without state support. The volunteer factor has also been decisive in American missionary work. With the exception of Puerto Rico and the Philippines after the 1898 war between the United States and Spain, there is no direct relationship between an American military presence and Christian mission. But things have not always been perceived in that way in the countries receiving U.S. missionaries. As Walls has remarked, "American missions have tended to think of themselves as non-political: how can it be otherwise if church and state live in different spheres? Non-Americans have seen continual political implications in their activities: how can it be otherwise if church and state inhabit the same sphere or at least overlapping spheres?"[30]

Many characteristics of missionary work from North America during the nineteenth and twentieth centuries may be seen at work in the Student Volunteer Movement for Foreign Missions (SVM). This movement was behind an increase in the American missionary force from 350 missionaries in 1890 to 4,000 in 1915. When the oldest Protestant missions gathered for a world consultation in Edinburgh (1910), the great architect of the meeting was John R. Mott, an American Methodist formed in the SVM. The famous watchword "the evangelization of the world in this generation" summarized the spirit and vision that Mott brought to that meeting.

The beginning of the SVM is usually traced back to a summer Bible school led by evangelist Dwight L. Moody at Mount Hermon in July 1886. Historian Dana Robert points to its spontaneous start: "The summer school did not begin with a foreign mission focus: Moody's interest in missions was limited primarily to home and urban revivalism. But the witness and prayers of a few collegians on fire for missions led to a general conflagration that burned throughout North America, Great Britain and Protestant Europe."[31]

The spontaneous movement among the students in North America had been manifest through the nineteenth century, beginning at the Haystack prayer meeting at Williams College in Massachusetts, August 1806. Four students from that meeting presented a petition to the General Assembly of the Congregational Churches on June 27, 1810, requesting the formation of a board of commissioners for foreign missions. The petition was adopted June 20, 1812. In this way, student initiative spurred the church in more than one denomination to become more active. This outburst of missionary concern was not something engineered at the headquarters of a powerful organization; God's Spirit was moving among people and forcing the institutionalized church to perceive its importance.

My study of the SVM and my observation and experience among university students around the world in the second half of the twentieth century have convinced me that the best of these movements share some distinctives: these are *spontaneous* movements; they have a definite *evangelical character*; they operate on the basis of a net of *personal relationships*; their leaders put an amazing *organizational ability* to the service of their vision; and the movements play a *fermenting role* as pioneers and catalysts in the renewal of the church.

As Christianity has expanded around the world in the twentieth century, local churches as well as youth movements have continued to be the source of missionary vocations. In my own limited experience within the IFES, I am acquainted with hundreds of missionaries whose call to service came at the time they were students in North America, Europe, Australia and New Zealand. More recently, I have seen a generation of new transcultural missionaries being raised from the ranks of evangelical student movements coming from young churches in places as diverse as Hong Kong, India, Nigeria, the Philippines, Korea, Japan, Brazil and Colombia. I know young Malaysian and Argentinean graduates who have taken secular positions in remote places of their own country in order to evangelize rural communities and to plant new churches. Many moving stories may be found in one of the best introductions to missionary work that I know, Ada Lum's *A Hitchhiker's Guide to Missions.*[32]

An overview of the history of missions is a picture of peaks and troughs. In twenty centuries the church has moved from being a sect of Judaism to becoming an immense global family of diverse peoples, cultures and languages who confess Jesus Christ as Savior and Lord. Ours is an age of globalization. Since the sixteenth century, Europe and later North America have been the Western centers from which the gospel has dispersed to other parts of the world. An honest reading of history shows just how true the words of the apostle Paul quoted at the beginning of this chapter are: the glorious treasure of the gospel has indeed been carried by earthly vessels. It will continue to be so because the Holy Spirit, who moves the church to become a missionary body, does not wait until perfect celestial instruments appear. Now that churches are being disestablished in the West, and Western culture is marked by a post-Christian ethos, a new opportunity is arising. Mehl has described it well: "Thus the churches are called to return to a situation that is closer to the primitive church than to the church of the Middle Ages. The *corpus Christi* ceases to be confused with the *corpus christianum,* and the church has become a differentiated society in relation to the total social body. Thus it is possible for the church to rediscover its specific nature."[33]

3

A Brave
New World Order

IQUITOS IS A FRONTIER CITY in the far eastern jungles of Peru. I have come to teach a course about Christian mission to a group of preachers and pastors from evangelical churches. Some of them have traveled for two days in small boats, following the course of the Amazon River's tributaries. During a pause I go to a public cabin to read my e-mail and catch up with news from friends and relatives. The attendant is wearing a shirt that advertises Pepsi, and before I get to my mail, Yahoo offers me a dating program in case I am lonely. There is a message from Bosnia, where my son Alejandro works with the Mennonite Economic Development Associates (MEDA). He writes about the course on financial management for small businesses that he is teaching, and he shares news from friends in Canada and Bolivia. He also refers to me a couple of questions from one of his colleagues who is in Uganda.

Some key principles of what Alejandro teaches he learned from his Mennonite supervisor, Cal, when he went to Santa Cruz, Bolivia, as a volunteer. Cal grew up on a farm in Ohio and learned those principles through a long Mennonite tradition forged over centuries of exile and persecution. Of course, Alejandro also learned at university about global markets and credit patterns, and he gained valuable experience from his seven years of work in Bolivia. As I read his e-mail in the heat of this Peruvian corner, for a moment I feel dazzled by the sudden awareness of how my son and I, and all these other people and places, are connected in time and space by the incredible web of the globalization process. As I consider Christian mission in the years to come I cannot avoid globalization as the cultural and social structure that surrounds my work, so I must try to understand how globalization will affect Christian mission and how better to prepare for it.

GLOBALIZATION

In 1955, during the Bandung conference of "nonaligned" nations, a French journalist coined the expression "Third World" to describe the non-Western and noncommunist nations in Asia, Africa and Latin America. After that year the way in which we looked at the world was influenced by the idea of three worlds: the Western capitalist world, the socialist world and the emerging "Third World" of new nations.

Most people living in western Europe and the United States used to think that their Western world was *the* Christian world. In many ways this perspective affected missionary concepts and practices. I met Catholic and Protestant missionaries in the 1960s who went to Latin America to "save it from communism." Well into the 1980s Ronald Reagan referred to the Soviet Union as "the evil empire," a phrase that implied that the capitalist West was the good empire. This bipolar perspective of the Cold War times that followed World War II was highly influential. With the collapse of the Soviet Empire in 1989, bipolar thinking became obsolete: there is now only one world power, the United States. Several regional alliances, such as the European Union or South-East Asia, constitute new poles, and as Robert Schreiter comments, "politically the world becomes a multipolar place that no one yet has been able to map persuasively."[1]

There is a growing awareness that the most recent form of capitalism is now embracing all nations on the planet through a sophisticated system of communication that takes the latest gadgets, habits and values of Western culture as merchandise to the most remote corners of the world. Even China, the giant whose future role in the world is unpredictable, or the Arab nations, which could become a powerful bloc animated by the Muslim faith, cannot escape this new trend. Jacques Attali wrote in 1991, "It is every day more and more evident that the central organizing principle of the future, whatever happens at the margins, will be economic. . . . The rule of military might that characterized the Cold War is being replaced by the reign of the market."[2] Like an irresistible wave, the market is the main force behind this process of globalization. The market is even giving a new language to the way some Christians in the United States speak about the church, since they speak about "marketing your church." Howard Snyder has aptly summarized this trend: "Global integration and networking are now the driving force in business and economics. The world is becoming one vast marketplace, not a patchwork of local markets. Economic integration on a world scale is reshaping society in a process that will reach well into the twenty-first century."[3] A crucial question to ask is how Christian mission is going to take place in this new world. Should Christian mission simply ride on the crest of the globalization wave?

Missionaries today go about their work making use of the globalization process just like missionaries of previous ages made use of the cultural and technological factors of their own time. For instance, in the field of Christian publishing, missionary linguists are working on the translation of the New Testament into an Indian language of Ecuador. A missionary aviation organization has flown the linguists to a remote village where they live and work. From there they will e-mail their drafts to their supervisor in Canada and discuss technical problems with him. When the manuscript is ready, the final layout of the book will be set by experts in Dallas, Texas, and then be sent by e-mail to Korea, where the books will be printed and later dispatched to Miami, the center from which they will be marketed in Ecuador. Distances are reduced: instant communication helps to accelerate the accomplishment of urgent goals; every step in a complex process may be referred to experts around the world; and when the time comes for a physical meeting of busy people, electronic communication helps everyone to attend better prepared for an important decision-making moment.

Missiologists who have reflected on this globalization process point to its ambiguities. Robert Schreiter, for instance, analyzes the modern values of "innovation, efficiency and technical rationality" that drive the global systems, but he states that though innovation connotes improvement, "without a clear goal [it] becomes change for its own sake, or change to create new markets or to stimulate desire."[4] This may be seen, for instance, in the way missionary organizations small and large constantly feel the pressure of the market to update the electronic and mechanical technologies in their offices. As a consequence their administrative costs keep spiraling, draining resources that could be invested in supporting more people for missions in new areas. Schreiter also writes, "Efficiency can mean less drudgery; but efficiency without effectiveness can become narrow and abstract, even deadly. Technical rationality has the advantage of providing clear purpose and procedure, but it can become profoundly dehumanizing."[5] I have observed this in the life of some missionaries and pastors in Latin America, the Middle East and eastern Europe. Managerial methods adopted by their leaders in their missions office at home bring pressures, because numbers of conversions are viewed as the standard of correct missionary practice. They have to produce a certain number of churches or conversions within a given time limit, and if they don't their failure is considered a sign of inefficiency, lack of faith or poor spirituality. This places intolerable burdens on them and is also destroying the ability of churches to develop pastoral responses to sweeping cultural transformations.

One of my students in Philadelphia was delighted when she was offered a position in a missionary organization. As a seasoned missionary

she looked forward to times of fellowship around projects of service in
the mission headquarters. After a few months of work she confided her
disappointment. There were too many rough edges and almost no times
of fellowship, because everybody was busy on their computers chatting
with people around the world. I have seen Latin American missionaries
who found the task of building fellowship with those around them day
after day extremely difficult; they turned instead to a selfish escape into
a fictitious "global village" thanks to the Internet.

What makes it arduous to critically evaluate the past and present as-
sociations of mission and globalization is the ambiguous relationship between Western missions and the modernization process that preceded
globalization. In the history of missions there is a point at which missionaries came to see themselves not only as evangelists but also as civilizers. A new stage in the process was reached when the expansion of
Europe overseas took place after Columbus came to the American continent in 1492. Iberian Catholic missions accompanied the process of
colonization that transported the feudal medieval social and economic
order that was disappearing in Europe to the Americas, some parts of Africa and the Philippines. Two centuries later, in the wake of British imperialism and the ideology in the United States of manifest destiny,
Protestant missions now had a modernizing component by their insis-
tence on Bible translation, literacy and leadership training for the laity,
and also by their use of modern medicine and the communication of basic technology. We have seen how today several aspects of globalization,
such as efficient communication at a global level or facilities for exchange within an increasingly connected economic system, are factors
that Christian mission may benefit from. However, an uncritical acceptance of modernization and globalization as supreme values would be
similar to the uncritical acceptance of the imperial order I described earlier in the Constantinian experience. They would become idols, *powers*
regarded as almost superhuman forces that cannot be reined in or even
challenged but are appeased or accepted as lords of our lives. Against

such idolatry a critical appraisal is imperative.

As it has been pointed out, the culture of globalization creates attitudes and a mental frame that may be the opposite of what the gospel teaches about human life under God's design. If mission simply rides on the crest of the globalization wave it might inadvertently change the very nature of the gospel. This is the warning that René Padilla presented forcefully in his paper at the Lausanne Congress of Evangelism in 1974. He expressed an awareness gained from the experience of evangelistic movements struggling to pattern their missionary activity according to biblical standards. He criticized the total identification of modern Western values (the American way of life) with the gospel, which was being propagated by many missionary organizations in the name of Christian mission. He called it "culture Christianity" and commented:

> In order to gain the greatest possible number of followers, it is not enough for "culture Christianity" to turn the gospel into a product; it also has to distribute it among the greatest number of consumers of religion. For this the twentieth century has provided it with the perfect tool—technology. The strategy for the evangelization of the world thus becomes a question of mathematical calculation.[6]

The criticism is still valid and is a solemn warning against some contemporary trends. For instance, precisely at the point in which religiosity has returned to be a mark of our postmodern culture, prayer for mission has been turned into an industry in which teachings and methodologies are packaged and marketed. Do not misunderstand me. I have a deep conviction that prayer is essential for mission, and I value new theological insights and methods that come from experienced people and the spiritual wisdom that comes from their practices. What I find questionable in the idea of "territorial spirits" and "spiritual warfare" is the quantifying rationality of American technological culture being uncritically applied even to the understanding of demonic activity and prayer. I now see nations at odds with the foreign policies of the United States or Europe being represented in maps as "windows," and I am told that through the techniques of spiritual mapping it is possible to detect within those nations a more intense demonic activity than in other parts of the earth. A thin line has been crossed when nationalism and patriotism lead us to demonize people and nations as enemies of our own nation. My suspicion is reinforced when I see this militaristic view of the world expressed also in worship and music that use almost exclusively the warlike language of the Old Testament. A strange form of Christian Zionism is sometimes propagated through evangelical media.

It is also true that the market forces that drive globalization make possible much of our daily life, as my son reminds me constantly. Bolivian farmers, for example, may grow beans instead of coca and sell their produce to Japan, while Korean workers may have a job because the trainers they make in their home industries can be exported to New York or Nairobi. My computer has some parts made in Japan and others made in Mexico or Malaysia. All of us from around the globe are connected in a web of relationships created by the reality of the market. Life today, including the life of Christians and missionaries, would not be possible without the human activity of buying and selling that is at the core of the market. But we are in danger of falling into a trap: having a view of a human being that makes money the measure of that person's worth. At the beginning of the modern age the French philosopher René Descartes made famous the saying "I think, therefore I am," but it seems that the contemporary paraphrase at this time of globalization is "I buy, therefore I am." That is the spirit of the age, and we must be careful not to become prisoners of it, lest we accept that human nature and happiness are totally dependent on the market. Jesus' warning is tremendously relevant now: "A man's life does not consist in the abundance of his possessions" (Lk 12:15).

CONTEXTUALIZATION

Contextualization is a word with a specific meaning in the field of mission studies. It refers to the way in which the text of the Bible or Christian theology is understood within its own cultural and historical context in order to apply its meaning in different contexts. (I shall deal with it further in chapter eight.) However, the term *contextualization* may also be understood in a more general way as a movement that seeks to affirm local cultures in their search for autonomy and full expression, as a reactive process in contrast to globalization.

If Christian mission has accompanied the globalization process and in a way contributed to it as we have seen, it has also played an important role in the general contextualization process. Through Bible translation, missions have contributed to the preservation, recognition and evaluation of native tongues and cultures. The historical significance of this movement has been the subject of research and writing by African scholar Lamin Sanneh. His thesis is that "particular Christian translation projects have helped to create an overarching series of cultural experiences with hitherto obscure cultural systems being thrust into the general stream of universal history."[7] Spanish missionaries of the sixteenth century, such as the Jesuit José de Acosta, wrote valuable geographical accounts and descriptions of the native cultures of the Americas that are still valid points of reference. Some aspects of the rich cultures of India, such as the Bengali language and literature, were first known and appreciated in Europe through the work of missionaries such as William Carey and his colleagues in Serampore. In their effort to understand the Indian mind in order to translate Scripture, they became conversant with Indian culture.

Conversely, Bible translation into the vernacular has been a decisive factor in the strengthening of a sense of identity and dignity of peoples and nations, thus preparing them to struggle against colonialism. On the basis of his research in Africa, Sanneh says, "When we look at the situation we are confronted with the paradox of the missionary agency promoting the vernacular and thus inspiring indigenous confidence at a time when colonialism was demanding paternal overlordship."[8] Bible translation, as well as the effort to plant indigenous churches and foster indigenous theologies, has facilitated for many peoples the affirmation of the local and the indigenous as a defense against the overwhelming weight of the globalization process.

At the same time, love for our own culture and language to the point of making them sacred and turning them into idols is also a trap to be avoided. In the middle of a social or economic crisis the contextualist reaction against globalization could take the destructive form of tribalism. Historian Justo González reminds us of events such as those following the collapse of the Soviet Empire and a variety of ethnic wars that developed in the Balkan peninsula. In African nations such as Somalia and Nigeria there were ethnic confrontations in 1991, while in cities of the United States like Los Angeles, African Americans and Korean Americans engaged in violent confrontations. González reminds us that "cultures and languages and nations and peoples are historical phenomena. They are part of this fallen creation, they carry in their very being the sign of sin."[9] If this is forgotten, love of our own language and culture may become demonic: "It is when we forget this that love of language and culture result in ethnic cleansing, in theories of supremacy, and in racial and cultural exclusivism."[10]

Foreign missionaries must always be aware that they may be carriers of the material tools or the intellectual vehicles of the globalization process. Respect for the local and the indigenous is indispensable, and missionaries can be trained to be sensitive to other cultures and critical of their own. Many times missionaries embody the tension between the global and the local, and need social and spiritual discernment that can be gained only through experience, in a spirit of love for the people and a pattern of mission modeled by the incarnational example of Jesus himself. Howard Snyder has expressed it forcefully: "The gospel is *global* good news. Thinking globally, God acted locally. The gospel is good news about personal, social, ecological and cosmic healing and reconciliation. It is good news to the whole creation—to the whole earth and in fact to the cosmos."[11] When the church is faithful to the Lord and to the gospel in its nature and life, the global and the local meet in the new creation.

A great challenge to Christian missionaries in the coming years will be how to remain first and foremost messengers of Jesus Christ and not just harbingers of the new globalization process. They will have to use the facilities of the system without being caught by the spirit of the system. This is a question not only for the missionaries from affluent societies but also for those from poorer societies who are tempted sometimes to rely mainly on the economic facilities and the technical instruments available to them. The biblical perspective on mission has a global vision and a global component that comes from faith in God the Creator and his intention to bless all of humankind through the instruments he chooses. At the same time, God is forming a new global people from races, cultures and languages spread over the whole earth, a people who cannot do less than have a global vision but who live their vision in the local situation where God has placed them. The contemporary globalization process has to be evaluated from that biblical perspective.

GROWTH OF POVERTY AND INEQUALITY

It has been pointed out that economics and the market are also motors of the globalization process. In different places and in many ways, globalization operating in countries or regions whose social structures have a tradition of corruption and inequality has accentuated social disparities. On the one hand, it has generated new wealth and unprecedented comfort, placing the most sophisticated technologies within the reach of the average citizen in rich nations and of the elites in poor nations. On the other hand, figures indicate that a larger proportion of people are being driven into extreme forms of poverty. An Indian missionary leader notes that in his country "some 300 million people guzzle Coke, even as 700 million struggle to find clean drinking water. These are India's poor. Absolute poverty has grown in the midst of globalization and the emergence of the new middle class."[12] According to Schreiter, "This is caused partially by global capitalism's quest for short term profit, a quest that precludes long term commitment to a people and a place; and partially by the destruction of traditional and small scale societies and economies by the centrality of the market."[13]

This process has brought uncertainty, suffering and decline in the quality of life for people whose welfare depends on public institutions, such as older and retired people, children, poor students or migrants. Christian missionaries become conversant with the subject because of their firsthand experience with the victims of this process. For instance, in most Latin American countries, long-term Christian endeavors such as theological education and institutional development necessary for the fulfillment of the church's mission have been affected by the collapse of local supporting structures, owing to growing unemployment brought by privatization of health, social security and education. Elsewhere, missions such as the Society for International Ministries (formerly Sudan Interior Mission, SIM) known for their commitment to evangelism, church planting and leadership training, have found it necessary to create an AIDS department to respond to an epidemic that has engulfed huge sections of the world, especially in Africa, and which affects mainly the poor.

Even in rich countries, accentuated social disparities have posed complex questions about mission for the church. Peter Drucker is an American economist who has mapped and evaluated the social transformation taking place in North America. He describes this process as the development of a postcapitalist society in which "knowledge workers" are replacing industrial workers. He stresses the fact that this shift to knowledge-based work brings enormous social challenges that will transform the lives of people, by the disappearance of old communities such as family, village and parish, for instance. For Drucker, neither government nor the employing organizations, the classic "two sectors" that hold power in the postcapitalist United States, are able to cope with the effects of this overwhelming social change, what he calls "social tasks of the knowledge society." These tasks include "education and health care, *the anomies and diseases of a developed and, especially, a rich society,* such as alcohol and drug abuse; or the problems of *incompetence and irresponsi-*

bility such as those of the underclass in the American city."[14]

Drucker places the agenda of assuming those tasks in the hands of what he calls "the third sector" of United States society, made up of churches and a myriad of voluntary organizations that he calls "para-churches" because they have modeled themselves on the nonprofit pattern provided by the churches. He assigns two responsibilities to this "social sector": "to create human health and well-being" and "to create citizenship." Of course, a presupposition behind Drucker's scheme is the tremendous volunteerism that characterizes American society and that has distinctly Protestant roots, though its contemporary manifestations may be secular in outlook and intention. His formula may not work in societies that have completely different structures, worldviews and attitudes. Volunteers of the kind Drucker proposes in his formula are usually people whose basic living needs are resolved and who enjoy a measure of leisure time.

THE POOR, GLOBALIZATION AND MISSION

One important development brought by the Lausanne movement after 1974 was the growing response of evangelicals to the challenge of poverty and injustice. There has been a significant multiplication of models of holistic mission that include a social component.[15] In Latin America, for instance, the number of street children who are victims of all forms of exploitation is the result of family disintegration, loss of basic Christian values and growing poverty. Many missionary projects have developed as a response, and there is now a network trying to coordinate them. Providing services for the material needs of people is in some places the only way missionaries can obtain a visa to enter a country. Mission projects of this kind are not just the result of a new awareness among Christians about a biblically based social responsibility; they're the inevitable response to worsening social conditions that have created many victims, who become a new challenge to Christian compassion. In many places in the twenty-first century, Christian compassion will be the only hope of survival for victims of the global economic process. The challenge for missionaries will be how to avoid the pitfalls of missionary paternalism and of the failed secular welfare system. Only the redemptive power of the gospel transforms people in such a way that it enables them to overcome the dire consequences of poverty.

Sociological studies of Christianity in the 1960s and 1970s were usually hostile toward churches. The scenario has changed today. As social planners and city governments acknowledge the problems generated by the current economic system, sociologists in places as distant as Philadelphia,[16] urban Brazil,[17] South Korea and South Africa[18] have come to see churches as the source of hope from which the urban poor gain strength, courage and a language to cope with poverty. Just as in New Testament times, even among the poorest the gospel brings a measure of prosperity because of its transforming effects. I shall deal more extensively with this theme in chapter nine.

However, there is also a significant missionary fact to which we must pay attention. It may seem a paradox from a purely human perspective. The poor of the world are the great missionary force of the present stage in mission history. In many nations around the world, people of all social classes are attracted to Jesus Christ and respond to his call. But it is especially among the poor that we find people open to the gospel and enthusiastic about their faith; churches are growing with astounding vitality in this world of poverty. While in some regions churches in other segments of society tend to decline, in Asia, Africa and Latin America evangelicals have found receptive hearts among the millions who have moved from rural areas to the cities. Even in North America and Europe popular forms of Protestantism are growing. I think there is a biblical precedent and many examples from history that prove the validity of what Howard Snyder says: "While the gospel is addressed to all people everywhere, it is especially a mission to the poor, the masses and the underclasses of the world. Though it excludes none who come to God with a 'humble and contrite heart,' the primary direction of its energy is toward the poor."[19] The churches of the poor have learned to respond to the urban challenge: they speak the language of the masses and offer fellowship in the impersonal city; they mobilize all church members for evangelism and give sacrificially for mission.

Moreover, as I have already pointed out, missionary initiative expressed in numbers of people volunteering for missionary work seems to be passing from North to South at a time when the South is increasingly poor. Within this context of poverty, two models of mission activity have developed that provide keys for the future. In the *cooperative model* churches from rich nations add their material resources to the human resources of the churches in poor nations in order to work in a third area. Some specialized evangelical organizations or ministries such as Youth With a Mission, Operation Mobilization and the International Fellowship of Evangelical Students have experience with this model, forming international teams to carry on transcultural missions in diverse settings. Several other missionary organizations are moving in this direction, but the model poses practical questions for which there are no easy answers, one of them being the raising of support for non-Western participants. The traditional, supranational Catholic missionary orders, such as Franciscans and Jesuits, provide an older and more developed example, facilitated by the vows of poverty, celibacy and obedience. They presuppose concepts of missionary vocation, church order and ministry totally different from the evangelical ones. The closest Protestant equivalent to these orders and their vows is the Salvation Army. I find significant the fact that this movement was created by a Methodist evangelist precisely as a response to the need to minister by word and deed to the urban poor in England at the end of the nineteenth century.

The *migration model* that has functioned admirably through the centuries is also an avenue for mission in our days. Migrants from poor countries who travel in search of economic survival carry the Christian message and missionary initiative with them. Moravians from Curazao moved to Holland, Jamaican Baptists emigrated to England, Haitian believers went to Canada, Filipina Christian women go to Muslim countries, and Latin American evangelicals are going to Japan, Australia and the United States. This missionary presence and activity has been significant, though it seldom gets into the records of formal, institutional missionary activity. Some denominational mission agencies, as well as faith missions, are trying to set up connections that will allow them to serve within the framework of this migration movement. They will need to exercise much care to avoid stifling the lay initiative and spontaneity that characterize it.

Spain has become one of the frontiers through which a flood of immigrants from Latin America and Africa try to enter Europe. Spain itself needs immigrants for its agriculture as Germany needs immigrants for its industry. In conversations with evangelical pastors in Spain I have heard several of them thanking God for the growing presence of Latin American believers who have the advantage of speaking the same language. The Latin Americans are a difficult challenge for Spanish churches, because many times they need economic help and solutions to their immigration problems, and it is not easy for old congregations to adapt to the presence of people who in some ways are culturally different. But pastors also acknowledge that the newcomers bring new missionary enthusiasm and energy, gifts that churches need in order to respond to the missionary challenge of postmodern Spain.

Existing missionary models among evangelicals have not been able to overcome the distances and barriers created by the comparative affluence of missionaries and agencies. The frequent tendency of Western mission agencies to bypass their indigenous partners and to perpetuate their own "independence" is an indication of failure, and growing poverty exposes that failure. The missionary dynamism of churches in the South could well be stifled and misdirected by an imitation of the expensive Western models of missionary organization. The future demands more models of nonpaternalistic, holistic missions. The incarnational approach modeled by Jesus and Paul is the key. Gross inequalities make partnership impossible. A church that lives comfortably in the post-Christian West is unable to respond to the pain and spiritual need of postmodern generations. It is interesting to see how spiritual vitality can foster a missionary stance in Western societies that expresses itself also in an ability to partner with churches abroad. Those who go to work as missionaries among the poor confess that many times they receive back the gift of joy from Christians who have an overflow of it in the midst of dire poverty and persecution.

One aspect of the globalization process affecting the brave new world order in which mission takes place in the twenty-first century is that the media propagates around the world the signs of the deep cultural change that has taken place in the West. There has been an erosion of Christian influence on forces that shape culture, such as legislation, education, the media or art. Alert Christians detected this in the first decades of the twentieth century, but it is now evident at first sight. We live in a post-Christian, postmodern world, a stark reality that missionaries cannot afford to ignore. We shall examine this situation in the following chapter.

4

Post-Christian
and Postmodern

I COME FROM A CHRISTIAN COUNTRY, SO THEY SAY. But a couple of years
ago, when fans of the Peruvian soccer team were waiting for an important match against the national team from Colombia, we watched on
our TV screens as witches and diviners of pre-Hispanic native religions
performed an elaborate ceremony offering sacrifices to Mother Earth
for the anticipated victory of the Peruvian team. There was neither
priest nor pastor to bless the game, though some of the players crossed
themselves before the match started. The way in which Christianity
has been displaced from its role of honor and influence in societies
where it was an official religion in the past has generated what we call
a post-Christian world. On the other hand, the renewed interest in all
kinds of religions, including those that existed before Christian missionaries appeared, can better be described as a sign of postmodernity.
Modern thinkers predicted the waning of religion with the rise of science and rationality. However, we now find ourselves in a more religious world. Enter any bookshop in Europe or North America and you
will find a large religious section in which a few Christian books will
often be outnumbered by books on spiritism, the New Age, Islam, Judaism and a variety of do-it-yourself manuals to cultivate the spiritual

life. What are some of the challenges of this new post-Christian, post-modern culture, which is propagated by the media on a global scale?

Before I consider the marks of this new culture it is important to remember that even within one country there is no cultural uniformity, and cultures are in a constant process of change. *Postmodern* and *post-Christian* are adjectives that describe basic trends in Western culture. Because of the expansion of Western culture during the nineteenth and twentieth centuries, through media and education for instance, any university graduate in any part of the world today has assimilated core elements from that Western culture. The technology that is part of our globalized world has Westernized habits, ways of relating, ways of moving around and communicating worldwide. Consequently, the cultural characteristics that embody the trends we call postmodern and post-Christian are spreading all over the world, and in many places different cultures coexist and interact in a process of transition.

For instance, in countries such as the Philippines, Peru or Nigeria, people in remote highlands or jungle areas live in a *premodern* culture. To survive the relentless advance of the Westernized part of their respective country they will need to learn basics of *modernity* such as literacy, the efficacy of vaccines or how to handle electricity. Willingly or unwillingly, some missionaries engaged in evangelism and church planting among such people are also the carriers of modernity—for example, those who provide Scriptures in native languages and teach people to read.

Yet in the modern capital cities of those countries we find among all social classes cultural traits we associate with *postmodernity*. Churches unable to understand postmodern youth are also unable to keep the new generations in their fold. I compare notes with my students from Myanmar, Ghana or India, and something similar is happening there. We need to understand these new cultural trends not only in the West but also globally.

Cultural analysis from the perspective of Christian mission operates with the basic assumption expressed clearly in paragraph ten of the Lausanne Covenant:

Culture must always be tested and judged by Scripture. Because man is God's creature, some of its culture is rich in beauty and goodness. Because he is fallen all of it is tainted with sin and some of it is demonic. The Gospel does not presuppose the superiority of any culture to another but evaluates all cultures according to its own criteria of truth and righteousness, and insists on moral absolutes in every culture.

This assumption is based on our Christian belief that human beings were gifted by their Creator with an ability to transform *natura* (nature) into *cultura* (culture). But there is also a historical reality to be taken into account—namely, the long, ambiguous relationship between Western culture and Christianity and the way that relationship influenced missionary work. The Covenant goes on to clarify that point: "Missions have all too frequently exported with the Gospel an alien culture and churches have sometimes been in bondage to culture rather than to the Scripture. Christ's evangelists must humbly seek to empty themselves of all but their personal authenticity in order to become the servants of others, and churches must seek to transform and enrich culture, all for the glory of God" (par. 10).

The post-Christian and postmodern trends in Western culture present us with an opportunity to follow this missionary agenda. The attitude expressed in the Covenant helps us to avoid the conservative proclivity to reject all cultural changes as detrimental to Christian life and to see instead the missionary opportunities that every new situation may bring. At the same time, it helps us engage in mission, going back to the fundamentals of the gospel, and disengage ourselves from those Western cultural trappings contrary to the gospel that, consciously or unconsciously, characterized mission during the imperial era in the nineteenth and twentieth centuries.

END OF CHRISTENDOM

Mission from the West in the past was done within a paradigm that presupposed the existence of a Christian social order, what is called Christendom. The world has changed. In the previous chapter I referred to unbalanced economic growth that has widened the gap between rich and poor. Such development could well be evidence of the degree to which Western culture has lost the veneer of the Christian values that it once respected. Chapter two examined how the position of the church in society evolved from the time that the emperor Constantine made Christianity official: "The church was blended into a half-civil, half-religious society, *Christendom*. It had covered a whole civilization with its authority, inspired a politic, and had become an essentially Western reality."[1] Christendom presupposed the dominance of Christianity in Western societies, as well as a certain degree of influence of Christian ideas and principles on the social life and international policies of nations. It is not difficult to agree with historian Kenneth Scott Latourette: "No civilization has ever incorporated the ideals of Christ."[2] But it is also important to remember that ideals such as fairness in national or international policies, or compassion expressed in foreign aid to poorer nations, are rooted in a long history of the influence of Christians on the development of legislation and the creation of institutions that embodied those ideals. Of course, history shows that many times, ruling classes within countries or governments failed to live up to their professed ideals in their international affairs. A post-Christian situation means that in the name of a pragmatism in which the market and profit determine the rules of the game, even the ideals are abandoned.

In this post-Christendom situation, Christians cannot expect society to facilitate through social mechanisms the kind of life that reflects the qualities of Christian ethics. Also within this situation, missionaries will have to expect less and less in terms of support or protection from their government as they travel and engage in mission. Legislation in the Western countries of Europe or North America ceases to be founded on Christian values. Today the Christian stance in the West has to become a missionary stance, in which to be a Christian is equivalent to being a "resident alien."[3] The same qualities required of pioneers who went to plant Christianity in the traditional mission fields have come to be required of Christians who stay at home in Western nations and want to be faithful witnesses of Jesus Christ. Coming from a life of missionary experience in Asia, Rosemary Dowsett has said it forcefully: "Neither the Lord Jesus himself nor the early church regarded minority status as abnormal. It was only with the advent of Christendom that the church was seduced into believing that she should exercise majority control by force, not faith (in parts of Europe we are still paying the price for that wrong turning)."[4] Missionaries have been inspired by the way in which Christians live their lives as a tiny minority in a hostile environment. Western Christians can learn much from Christians who daily have to practice an alternative lifestyle.

I have already mentioned movements that minister among young people and students, movements that have been more open to taking risks by creating models of sensitive multicultural missionary teams. Participants have been able to look at their own culture from a critical distance. This has been facilitated also by the mobility and simple lifestyle of the teams. Through experience and reflection in the light of God's Word this has been an important training ground for mission. I believe that this type of experience gives participants a taste of some of the positive characteristics of the traditional monastic orders that have remained in the Catholic Church as instruments for mission across cultural and social frontiers. Facilities for travel allow this educational process to be experienced through short-term visits involving immersion in other cultures, and fellowship with brothers and sisters in Christ in other lands. However, much care has to be exercised to avoid turning this opportunity into one more form of selfish tourist consumerism.

A POSTMODERN CULTURE

Not only is Christianity itself being rejected in contemporary Western societies, Christian values too are coming under fire. The rejection of a Christian ethos has to be understood within the wider frame of an attitude that also rejects ideologies and worldviews shaped by the Enlightenment, usually known as modernity. Now we see in the West the rise of a culture with attitudes that might be described as postmodern because they revolt against some of the marks of modernity. Thus we witness the ascendance of feeling and the revolt against reason, the revival of paganism in elements such as the cult of the physical, the search for ever more sophisticated forms of pleasure, and the ritualization of life. Sports and popular artistic shows take the shape of religious celebration and replace church services as a way to provide relief from the drudgery of routine work and duty.

An important aspect of postmodernity is the glorification of the body. Postmodern culture depicts the body in all forms and offers thousands of products to beautify, perfume, modify, improve and perfect it, even to the point of promising ways to overcome the inroads of aging. There are products, methods and stimuli for enhancing physical pleasure in all its forms. This search for pleasure has become a mark of contemporary life that, coupled with the hopelessness brought about by the collapse of ideologies, becomes pure and simple hedonism. The media portrays this hedonistic way of life and thought, and propagates it across the globe. Incitement to expensive pleasure fills the screens of TV sets in poor societies, and young people especially crave for the symbols and instruments of a sophisticated, hedonistic West while lacking some of the basic necessities of life such as adequate housing and running water.

An important mark of modernity was that its myths provided hope and a sense of direction to the masses. Some of us remember well how the Marxist dream of a classless utopia fostered political militancy in several generations of students who were ready to give their lives for the cause of the proletariat. When I attended high school we were required to memorize the political liberal discourses of the French Revolution, with its dreams of unlimited progress. Later Marxism arrived, and the words of Argentinean medical doctor Che Guevara, painted on the walls of the University of Córdoba in Argentina, come to mind as an illustration: "What does the sacrifice of a man or a nation matter if what is at stake is the destiny of humankind?" A mark of postmodernity is the loss of those utopian dreams. Nowadays, politicians, teachers of philosophy and historians seem not to have a clue about the direction in which history is moving—and it does not seem to matter anymore. The philosophy of life of postmodern urban youth is embodied in words the apostle Paul quotes from Isaiah to describe the materialism of his own day:

Let us eat and drink,
for tomorrow we die. (1 Cor 15:32)

Such materialism lies behind the attitude that turns consumption into the main interest of the average citizen. The incredible abundance of consumer goods generated by the modern economy is met by the passion for buying and using—the ideology of consumerism. The great shopping centers, open seven days a week, have become the new temples of a postmodern religion, and it is not difficult to detect the vacuum in the lives of its worshipers. Jacques Attali describes these people as modern nomads who, with Walkmans, laptops and cell phones, "roam the planet seeking ways to use their free time, shopping for information, sensations and goods only they can afford, while yearning for human fellowship and the certitudes of home and community that no longer exist because their functions have become obsolete."[5]

Statements like this, from secular sources, about the human condition in the postmodern culture come close to the theological description of the symptoms of the fallen condition of human beings. Postmodern literature in both the North and the South evidences the cynicism and bitter disillusion accompanying the end of modern myths and ideologies. In affluent postmodern societies, people like this constitute the "unreached peoples" who challenge Christian compassion. Prayer is required here, along the lines of what Jesus taught us when he looked at the "harassed and helpless" masses of his day (Mt 9:36). Compassion and prayer must have priority over a kind of triumphalistic apologetics that seems to be saying "I told you so" from the distance of a self-righteous aloofness. Missionary obedience at this frontier is mandatory for evangelical churches and is as urgent as missionary obedience to go to "unreached peoples" in exotic jungles or remote rural areas.

RELIGIONS OLD AND NEW

Modernity in both its liberal and Marxist clothes operated with the "enlightened" presupposition that religion was in the process of waning away. During the first part of the twentieth century, Christian thinkers were confronted in cultural circles by a hostile rationalism nourished by the three "masters of suspicion": Marx, Nietzsche and Freud. From the perspective of Christian mission, the return of an attitude of openness to the sacred and the mysterious seemed at first sight a sign of improvement. Soon, however, it became evident that Christians were being confronted with a new and subtler challenge. Our way of communicating and defending the gospel needed serious refurbishing because the plausibility, authenticity and quality of our faith were now being questioned from a different angle.

By the 1970s, as a student evangelist on campuses in Canada, Chile, Brazil and the Philippines I had a chance to engage with students who showed this new openness to the religious. I remember a physics student in Mexico who shouted at me during the question time in a lecture at the National Autonomous University of Mexico, "We are not anymore interested in Marx and how to change the world. What I would like to know is if the Christian faith has a method for developing the potential of the spiritual forces inside me." In many cases this new attitude allowed Christians to demonstrate a freer and uninhibited expression of their faith through prayer, song and drama in the open air. I found myself involved in dialogues with people whose language was strangely similar to the language of some forms of evangelicalism: joy in the heart; a feeling of self-realization; a sense of peace and harmony; a feeling of goodwill toward human beings, animals and planet earth. However, when I addressed specific issues such as suffering, death, compassion, final hope, failure and sin, this new religious mood changed. When I talked of the cross, evil, sin, redemption and Christ, I could see hostility developing against what was considered my exclusivism and intolerance.

The new attitude toward religion and the proliferation of religious practices has to be understood as part of the revolt against modernity. The modern ideologies of indefinite progress and social utopia were actually myths that attracted and mobilized the masses for action. Their collapse has brought awareness of a vacuum and disillusionment about the ability of human reason to give meaning to life and provide answers for deep existential questions. This is at the root of the search for alternatives, for an ability to handle mystery, for contact with the occult, for a connection with extrarational forces that may influence the course of events in individual lives as well as in communities and nations.

It is helpful to remember that in the days of the New Testament, the message of Jesus Christ confronted the challenges of Greek philosophy and Roman politics but also the questions that came from the mystery religions that pervaded the ideas and practices of popular culture. Mystery religions in the first century claimed to help human beings with their daily problems, to give them immortality and to enable them to share their life with the god. They promised cleansing to deal with guilt, security to face fear of evil, power over fate, union with gods through orgiastic ecstasy, and immortality.[6] The way in which the apostolic message and practice developed in the New Testament was the response to these needs of the human heart, stemming from the basic fact of Jesus Christ.[7]

Missionaries today are being driven to restudy the New Testament teaching about religiosity as well as about the presence and power of the Holy Spirit. Communication technology and techniques as well as an intellectually reasonable faith are not enough. Spiritual power and disciplines such as prayer, Bible meditation and fasting are necessary for mission across the new religious frontier. Evangelicals must be open to the ministry of people who are gifted to minister in these areas. On the other hand, the apostle Paul, writing to the Corinthians, recognized that there could be worldliness, abuses and manipulation even within a context of spectacular spiritual gifts. Croatian theologian Peter Kuzmič said at the Lausanne II evangelical congress in Manila, "Charisma without character leads to catastrophe." Those of us who work in theological education and training for mission in North America have become aware of the importance of spiritual formation for ministers and missionaries. A change of mind is necessary at this point, as missiologist Jim Pluedemann has expressed with precision: "The dominant current paradigm for mission is that of an efficient machine. Spiritual formation is neglected because it does not easily fit the assembly-line paradigm. The factory paradigm encourages missionaries to set objectives for mere outward behavior. It is primarily interested in quantities."[8] He emphasizes that spiritual growth involves a process that takes place inside a person; it is not something that can be measured, controlled or predicted. "The best way to facilitate spiritual formation is to make available the means of grace that God uses to promote the process of maturity, . . . the Word of God, the Spirit of God and the people of God."[9]

If we accept the fact that the West, namely Europe and North America, is to be considered a mission field, we also must accept as valid the search for a missionary approach that will take seriously the cultural context of that mission field. A missiologist who has done much work on the subject from a church-growth perspective is George Hunter III, who says that the cultural barrier between the churches and unchurched people is the largest single cause of the decline of European Christianity and a bigger problem for mainline American Christianity. Hunter poses a dramatic question: "The U.S.A. is a vast secular mission field with many cultures and subcultures. Are we imaginative enough and compassionate enough to sponsor and unleash many forms of indigenous Christianity in this land?"[10] He thinks that the so-called apostolic congregations proliferating in North America are responding adequately to this missionary challenge; among others, he mentions Saddleback

Church in Orange County, California. This church and others, such as Willow Creek in Illinois, are the megachurches that have developed in the most recent decades.

These churches show some of the marks of classical evangelicalism in their doctrine and evangelistic concern, but they studiously avoid names that would indicate a denominational origin in any of the well-known mainline Protestant churches. Their success seems to be related to their ability to respond positively to the needs, attitudes and outlook generated by the market culture in a postmodern society. Hunter emphasizes that in their liturgy, their style of preaching, their way of organizing the participation of people through small groups, and their comfortable atmosphere in terms of dress and lifestyle, these churches have removed the cultural barriers that have kept people away from the traditional churches. They have been successful at "marketing their church," and through media and missionary action they are starting to reproduce themselves or to influence traditional evangelical churches outside the United States.

There is a growing number of similar "postdenominational" churches in other parts of the world. In Latin America, for instance, some Catholic charismatic groups have become independent churches that show in their preaching, lifestyle and liturgy some of the marks of the middle-class Catholic culture from which they proceed. They avoid the language and worship style of the traditional evangelical churches, as well as some of the marks of the evangelical subculture in terms of dress code or religious language. Their teaching emphasizes prosperity and well-being. The theological claims of these postdenominational churches to be an "apostolic" movement sent by God to renew his church must be evaluated on the basis of biblical teaching and theological discernment. However, their ability to attract unchurched people poses a missiological question that has to be taken seriously in the post-Christian, postmodern world.

We have to acknowledge that Protestants in general, and evangelicals in particular, have emphasized *true doctrine* as a mark of the church, but they have been weak in their understanding of the importance of *ritual and symbol* as well as *church structure* for the discipleship process and the growth of people in their faith, and for the communication of the gospel. The evangelical emphasis on preserving the integrity of the faith has been important in the recent history of missions. However, there has sometimes been a misplaced zeal to preserve cultural forms of previous generations with no regard for cultural changes. There has been a tendency to preserve social conventions typical of the middle-class worship styles that were successful in past generations: music that accompanied the revivals of previous centuries, dress styles that became inflexible "approved standards." Missionaries have sometimes transmitted this attitude to churches in other cultures, creating their own cultural barriers that keep people away from an honest confrontation with the gospel. While we may be critical of some theological tenets of the so-called apostolic churches, we can learn from their ability to overcome cultural barriers and attract people of the postmodern generation.

OLD RELIGIONS AND FUNDAMENTALIST WARS

Besides the new religiosity there is the resurgence of old religions. In the streets of London, Madrid, Philadelphia or Los Angeles, mosques and Hindu temples increasingly fill the cityscape, not as exotic casino ornaments but as places of worship for communities that sometimes outdo Christians in their missionary zeal. With the end of Christendom many societies face the thorny issue of religious pluralism. The West, with its Protestant ideals and practice of democracy and tolerance, was intellectually prepared for it, but in countries where Catholicism and the Orthodox Church are the religious mainstay, pluralism is difficult to come to terms with. All Christians, however, are faced with the need to review their attitudes, and a more alert form of apologetics must be matched by spiritual discernment.[11]

One of the most significant trends in recent years is the resurgence of Islam, making it one of the greatest missionary challenges of today. From the viewpoint of influence on society and use of mechanisms of social control, Islam is now a rival of Christianity in Indonesia, several sub-Saharan countries, the Middle East and even the heart of cities in Europe and the United States. Recently Nigeria and Indonesia, countries in which the growth of Christianity or Islam has immediate political consequences, witnessed repeated violent confrontations between Christians and Muslims. The terrorist attacks of September 11, 2001, on New York and Washington, D.C., have not only unleashed a war but posed questions of international politics and cultural trends that will affect Christian mission for decades to come. Most Christians today would like to avoid a repetition of the crusades, but in spite of the decline of Christendom and the avowed pluralism of the West, some leaders of Western nations are still attracted by the old rhetoric of the crusades to rally support for their wars.

Unfortunately many Christians still operate with those categories. I attended the Urbana 90 Student Mission Convention when the airwaves were charged with propaganda preceding the Gulf War. One of the speakers presented the challenge of unevangelized areas, most of which were Muslim countries, and labeled them as "creative access" places. I was shocked by the use of military imagery and the nationalistic implications of his speech. To my relief, the next morning I found I was not alone in my protest. An associate member of the staff of InterVarsity Christian Fellowship wrote in a letter to the conference newspaper, "From a position of power and wealth we divide the world according to our categories and strategize how we will conquer. Foreign policy couched in spiritual conflict terms. Militaristic attitudes baptized in the name of Christ. Haven't we learned anything from history?"[12]

A more difficult reality to face is the phenomenon of *fundamentalism*. This term was coined to refer to the conservative reaction against theological liberalism among Protestants in the United States at the beginning of the twentieth century. What started as a theological effort to reformulate and defend the fundamentals of evangelical faith became dominated by what Carl Henry calls "a harsh temperament, a spirit of lovelessness and strife." Its anti-intellectualism degenerated into "a morbid and sickly enthusiasm,"[13] and it became a reactionary cultural phenomenon associated with the defense of a conservative political agenda in the United States. It was often associated with racism, nationalism, blind anticommunism and the arms race.

When a resurgent Islam took power in Iran in the 1980s, this movement and the religious-political groundswell that followed in several other countries of the Middle East and North Africa came to be known as Muslim fundamentalism. Around the same time, Protestant fundamentalists in the United States came to political prominence through the Moral Majority. It is this reaction against modernity and secularism from a conservative alliance of religious conviction and political interests that today is known as fundamentalism. There is Hindu fundamentalism in India, Jewish fundamentalism in Israel and the United States, and Catholic fundamentalism in Mexico and Argentina. Other religions such as Buddhism have also taken fundamentalist forms. From a missiological perspective the problem is the confusion this might create. Protestant fundamentalism in the form of religious-political alliances, such as the media empires of Pat Robertson and Jerry Falwell, intend to mix evangelism with the promotion of a variety of political causes in different parts of the world.

Is the situation of Islam after the September 11 terrorist attacks one of greater strength or greater weakness? The attacks and their aftermath have revealed the divisions in Islam in relation to the way Muslims face modernity. Will a majority of leaders of Islam eventually distance themselves from the fundamentalist tendencies among their followers? The first reaction of Muslim intellectuals and leaders in the United States and Europe was to stress that suicidal terrorism was not true to the teachings of Islam. What is tragic from the perspective of Christian mission is the negative historical record of countries calling themselves "Christian" with regard to international politics in relation to peoples and nations of the Muslim faith. We must remember that horrible events of the twentieth century such as the communist terror or the Holocaust were not perpetrated by Muslims.

The Lausanne movement consultation "Gospel and Culture" in 1978 had a special section on Islam. The final document, known as the Willowbank Report, has recorded the concerns of participants about the issue: "On the one hand a resurgence of Islamic faith and mission is taking place in many lands, on the other hand there is a new openness to the gospel in a number of communities which are weakening their ties to traditional Islamic culture."[14] The document reminds readers of the need to recognize distinctive features of Islam that provide a unique opportunity for Christian witness, and that "although there are in Islam elements which are incompatible with the gospel, there are also elements with a degree of what has been called 'convertibility.'" The conclusion, in view of the troubled past, is challenging: "The crux of a lively, evangelizing sense of responsibility towards Muslims will always be the quality of Christian personal and corporate discipleship and the constraining love of Christ."[15] This coincides with what I have learned from evangelical missionaries I have known, such as William Miller, Dennis Clark, Margaret Wynne and Phil Parshall, who worked among Muslims. They taught me that the keys to missions in the Muslim world are humility and a disposition to serve, patterned on Jesus' attitude of readiness to take up the cross and suffer, and a respectful acquaintance with the Muslim faith.

5

We Believe in a Missionary God

VISHAL MANGALWADI ENDS ONE OF HIS "Letters to a Postmodern Hindu" as follows:

> Your son's suffering is a challenge to God. India's brokenness is an even greater challenge to Him. What is He going to do about His creation which is now so ugly and so painful? Satan used man and woman to spoil God's creation. God responds by sending His men and women—the missionaries—to begin to restore what has now become so ugly.

The letters were addressed to Arun Shourie, a social activist who wrote a bitter critique of Christian missionary presence in India, past and present. Mangalwadi himself is an evangelical Indian, a social reformer and author who lives in Mussoorie, where he leads the Association for Comprehensive Rural Assistance. Among the reasons for Shourie's criticism of Christian mission is his eighteen-year-old child's suffering, caused by brain injury, which Shourie cannot reconcile with the idea of a compassionate and powerful God. Mangalwadi writes at another point:

> I am one of your admirers, Mr. Shourie, because you have fought (so brilliantly) against moral degeneration in India. It would be tragic if you too

were to surrender before evil and become a true Buddhist—concluding that evil and suffering cannot be fought against because they are intrinsic to this world. No, they ought not to be there. They are against God's will. Therefore we must fight on. One implication of the view that suffering is against God's will is that we can enlist God's help against it.[1]

GOD CHOOSES AND GOD SENDS:
WE BELIEVE IN A MISSIONARY GOD

The biblical conviction that God is active in the world, active in human history through people he calls and sends, is at the heart of mission. At the time of his conversion to Jesus Christ, the famous French mathematician Blaise Pascal wrote his well-known *Memorial*, found on a piece of paper sewn into his coat when he died: "Fire! God of Abraham, God of Isaac, God of Jacob not of the philosophers and the scholars." This contrast between two visions of God, which Pascal expressed and Mangalwadi reiterated in a simple but powerful way, points to the fact that Christians believe in a God who has revealed himself in history. First, God wants to be known and does not remain hidden, in contrast to the idea of a God who hides himself away in mystery so that only a select elite may approach him. Second, God has revealed himself in and through historical events, and supremely in Jesus Christ, the One he sent as the clearest revelation of his love and saving purpose.

This is the God who called Abraham out of Ur and sent him into an unknown land, promising that from that old man and his wife a nation would be born, a human family through whom God wanted to bless all families on earth (Gen 12:1-3). God's saving purpose was universal in its dimension, but he chose one man and one people to accomplish it. The God of Abraham and of Jesus Christ is not, therefore, a local totem who wants to favor one clan for its own sake. Rather, he is the Creator of humankind and wants to bless all peoples within this human family. To fulfill his universal purpose, however, he began with one family. This mystery of election, that the blessing for all requires the choosing of one as the instrument, is a scandal to human logic. As Newbigin has pointed out so forcefully, the logic of election corresponds to the biblical understanding of human beings that always sees human life in terms of relationships: "There is, there can be no private salvation, no salvation which does not involve us with one another. In order to receive God's saving revelation we have to open the door to the neighbor whom he sends as his appointed messenger."[2]

As a man chosen by God, Abraham enters into a covenant with the Creator. God calls, and Abraham hears the call and obeys it; he acts in faith, believing that God will do what he has promised. Therefore, the apostle Paul says, Abraham is the father of all those who respond to God in faith, not only of those who are biologically (or ethnically) descendants of Abraham: "He is the father of us all" (Rom 4:16). Is it not significant that three great religious traditions that have had a decisive role in human history trace their ancestry—in a way their existence—back to this act of obedience of Abraham? The faith of Abraham included his willingness to walk in the way of the Lord. Abraham's descendants became a nation constantly called to live a life that would illustrate God's purpose in creating humankind, a life of obedience to the law of the Lord. They were to be a "holy people," in other words, a "separate" nation. Egypt was a furnace in which, through suffering, the nation was forged. Then, after their miraculous deliverance in which they came to know God as the One who liberated them from oppression and injustice, the pilgrimage in the desert was also a formative time before they came into possession of the Promised Land. The biblical story depicts how the nation was sometimes faithful and at other times unfaithful to their covenant with God. It also shows how there were faithful people from the nation who became a blessing to other nations, such as Joseph in Egypt, Daniel in Babylon and Nehemiah in Persia. When military defeat and exile resulted in the breakdown of the nation, the prophets interpreted history from the perspective of God's purpose of universal blessing and his design for Israel.

God both chooses and sends. Bible men and women—such as Abraham and Sarah, Joseph, Moses, Jeremiah, Esther, John the Baptist, Peter, and Paul, to mention just a few—had lives marked by a clear sense of being *called and sent*. And of course, Jesus our Lord set his own life and ministry within this perspective. At the beginning of his mission in the synagogue of Nazareth he read the passage from Isaiah,

> The Spirit of the Lord is on me,
>> because he has anointed me. . . .
> He has sent me. (Lk 4:18)

As he approached the end he said, "Now I am going to him who sent me" (Jn 16:5); and after he rose again from the dead he also commissioned his disciples, "As the Father has sent me, I am sending you" (Jn 20:21). Being called and sent by God is the essence of mission. Lucien Legrand reminds us that

> the word "mission" can boast a respectable biblical pedigree. "Mission" means "sending." This is the idea expressed by the Greek verbs *pempein*, to "send" (used 79 times in the New Testament) and *apostellein*, to "send forth" (used 137 times, counting the occurrences of *exapostellein* in the sense of sending). The "missionary," the one sent, is the *apostolos* (79 times), and the apostle's task is the *apostolē* (4 times).[3]

The mission to which God sends those he chooses is always a "mission impossible," possible only because God will act in order to accomplish his purpose. Again, this is a pattern we see throughout the Scriptures. To begin with, Abraham, "the one to whom God has proclaimed that he will become a great people, has an infertile wife, and when his child is born miraculously, he receives the order to sacrifice him."[4] At pivotal moments in their lives, Joseph and Moses, as much as Paul or Peter, have to face the impossibility of their mission. Jesus himself is born from a miraculous work of the Holy Spirit. In its way of telling the stories the Bible seems to be warning us against triumphalist attitudes that will give glory to the human agent. The most eloquent in this regard was Paul the missionary. Writing to the Corinthian church, which he founded and in which people are now questioning his authority, Paul reminds them that he does not need letters of recommendation, because the members of that church are themselves his letter: "You yourselves are our letter. . . . You show that you are a letter from Christ, the result of our ministry, written not with ink but with the Spirit of the living God" (2 Cor 3:2-3). And immediately he goes on to clarify: "Not that we are competent in ourselves to claim anything for ourselves, but our competence comes from God" (2 Cor 3:5). A few paragraphs later, writing about the glory of God's power in action he goes on to state, "But we have this treasure in jars of clay to show that this all-surpassing power is from God and not from us" (2 Cor 4:7). All glory has to be given to God; Paul wants to avoid glorifying himself or any other human instrument.

Missionary enthusiasm and activism can sometimes take us to the point of acting as if mission is a purely human enterprise subject to human calculations. Some years ago when a well-known evangelist was coming to the city of Philadelphia, a person from the advance work team said during one of the training sessions, "We estimate that x percent of the attendants will make decisions, therefore . . ." Such a statistical approach shocked my Latin American and African students, to whom the technological and pragmatic approach of American culture was still new and unusual. To keep an attitude of alertness to God's initiative in mission, missionary life must include the discipline of continuous exposure to his Word, contemplation of Jesus as model and humble dependence on the Holy Spirit in prayer. When we recover a biblical vision we experience the wonder of being invited to enter God's plan, which has far broader implications than choosing a career or going on a pleasant vacation abroad. We experience the sense of the sacred, the otherness of God and our own inadequacy that makes us say, as Moses said before the burning bush, "Who am I?" (Ex 3:11); or we gain an awareness of our sinfulness, as Peter exclaimed when Jesus climbed into his boat, "Go away from me, Lord; I am a sinful man!" (Lk 5:8); or we fall to the ground and ask, like Saul did when he encountered Jesus in the blinding light on the Damascus road, "Who are you, Lord?" (Acts 22:8).

MISSIONARY EXISTENCE BETWEEN TWO POLES: OBEDIENCE AND DISOBEDIENCE

Some psalms from Israel's hymnal, which emphasize God's action in favor of his people, appear to be deeply ethnocentric. In the psalms of Zion (e.g., Ps 46; 48; 76; 84; and esp. Ps 87) is a vision of all the nations coming to Jerusalem, which becomes like the center of the universe, and paying tribute to Israel. But there are also psalms that show an understanding of the blessings for Israel as blessings that will reach all nations. For instance, Psalm 67:1-2 says:

> May God be gracious to us and bless us
>   and make his face shine upon us,
> that your ways may be known on earth,
>   your salvation among all nations.

Walter Kaiser reminds us that the risen Christ's answer to the disciples' question about Israel (Acts 1:7-8) has echoes of the language of this psalm:[5]

> God will bless us,
>   and all the ends of the earth will fear him. (v. 7)

There is in the psalms a certain polarity between the sense of being bearers of a unique and special blessing from God and the sense of obligation to be a light for the nations.[6] Israel's exile among other nations could be interpreted as a means by which God scattered Israel to the ends of the earth to prepare the way for the coming of the Messiah. When the gospel of Jesus Christ started to spread through the Roman Empire, the first point of contact of the missionaries was the Jewish synagogue, where people met around God's Word. That Word had already been translated into Greek, which was the common language of the empire. In a way, then, the missionary process started with the Jewish exile.

Thus in the Old Testament as well as in the New runs the self-revelation of the God who wants to bless and save all human beings because he loves his whole creation. The compassion of God and his concern for all humankind in judgment as well as in grace is the note that marks the teachings of the prophets, and without it we can understand neither the existence of Israel nor the mission of Jesus Christ. But through the pages of Scripture runs also the story of a tension within the people of God, between their missionary existence to be a blessing to all nations and all peoples, and the temptation to selfishly enjoy the blessings of their privileged position and refuse to be obedient to God's purpose.

Luke describes this tension in his Gospel and in the book of Acts. The strong denunciation by Jesus in the parable of the barren fig tree (Lk 13:1-9) comes as the culmination of a mounting tension between the established religion of Israel at that point and Jesus, who is the fulfillment of the prophetic promises and who is, ironically, rejected by the most religious. Luke places that rejection at the very start of Jesus' ministry, in the synagogue of Nazareth. Jesus is offered the Scripture scroll and from it reads a section of Isaiah's prophecy, a section filled with a sense of call and vocation for mission:

> The Spirit of the Lord is on me,
>> because he has anointed me
>> to preach good news to the poor.
> He has sent me to proclaim freedom for the prisoners
>> and recovery of sight for the blind,
> to release the oppressed,
>> to proclaim the year of the Lord's favor. (Lk 4:18-19)

"He has anointed me" and "He has sent me" both refer to being chosen, being prepared, being sent, which are at the heart of mission. And having captured the attention of the people, Jesus makes a forceful statement: "Today this scripture is fulfilled in your hearing" (Lk 4:21). The audience is enthusiastic and "amazed at the gracious words" that proceed from his lips (Lk 4:22). However, when Jesus starts to remind them that in the past God chose to manifest himself to people outside Israel, to Phoenicians and Syrians, an instantaneous and dramatic rejection follows. Jesus is driven out of town and almost killed.

The rejection of salvation for the Gentiles in the synagogue of Pisidian Antioch (Acts 13, esp. vv. 42-52) is another instance of that tension. It is the first intentional missionary journey on which the church of Antioch, in obedience to the call of the Holy Spirit, has sent Paul and Barnabas. The two apostles preach in the synagogue, showing how Jesus was the fulfillment of God's promises to Israel. Jews as well as "devout converts to Judaism" are highly receptive, and a week later a large crowd, "almost the whole city," gathers to hear them. But Luke reports that "when the Jews saw the crowds, they were filled with jealousy" (Acts 13:43-45). González comments, "The text does not tell us why they were jealous, but one surmises that they were disturbed that what up to that point had been their exclusive property (which they shared with a few proselytes who adjusted to what they said) was now open to the entire city."[7]

In view of the resistance of these Jews, Paul takes upon himself and Barnabas the obedience to the missionary purpose of God, using as a paradigm the following statement from Isaiah:

> I have made you a light for the Gentiles,
>   that you may bring salvation to the ends of the earth. (Acts 13:47)

For the apostle Paul and for Luke, the recorder of his missionary journeys, this attitude of the Jews was a refusal to accept their own mission. God's purpose was unfolding before their eyes, yet they were "jealous" and wanted to limit him to being the deity of the Jewish people only, their own national God.

An exaggerated sense of separateness, an intense desire to preserve their cultural identity, a narrow and ethnocentric understanding of God's purpose, a conformist attitude toward established religion—all of these elements may explain the mystery of Israel's rejection of Jesus Christ not only in New Testament times but in the last two thousand years of history. To what degree cultural factors played a role in New Testament times is evident in the book of Acts. Within the church of Jerusalem it is clear that the contact with "the other," the one who is different, is what becomes intolerable to the Jews. They reproach Peter because of the actions involved in his first missionary foray into Gentile territory: visiting and eating with uncircumcised men (Acts 11:1-4). Indeed Peter had been able to take such steps in mission only after a great personal struggle to align himself with the purpose of the missionary Christ. On the other hand, the church at Antioch—located at the crossroads of commerce and cultures, with a culturally and ethnically mixed makeup and leaders who spend time in worship and expectant prayer (Acts 13:1-3)—is obedient to God's call and open to the surprises of transcultural mission. Antioch becomes the base for the initial missionary journeys of the apostles entrusted with taking the gospel to the Gentile world.

The reluctance of God's people to obey when they are sent is also evident in the twenty centuries of Christian history. While Christians confess in their creeds and their worship that they believe in a God who loves the world so much that he sent his Son to reveal his love and accomplish salvation for all humankind, frequently they do not care much about what has to be done today to demonstrate that love and to communicate this good news to the world. Thousands of churches carry on "business as usual" without ever asking the simple question, "Why has God placed us as a community, at this time, in this neighborhood, in this city, in this country, in this world?" Almost always those who are vitally interested in mission are a small minority in churches and denominations. Many times in history, churches that were great and powerful disappeared because they lost the sense of mission. They became so identified with their culture that they lost any sense of mission to it, any ability to be prophetic in the name of Jesus Christ. At other times they became so absorbed by the routine of their own needs and interests that they lost a vision of the needs of others for whom they could have been God's messengers.

Historians recall with sadness that the churches in North Africa, so gifted and powerful in the second and third centuries, identified too closely with the Latin culture of the colonial elite of which they were a part and did not care to evangelize the local native population or to translate the Bible into their language. They became comfortable and isolated. The founding generation had withstood courageously the trial of bloody persecution from the Roman Empire, but when the Muslim advance subjected the new generations to the subtle persecution of becoming second-class citizens, they could not survive.

SPIRITUAL REVIVAL AND MISSION

Mission exists because God is a missionary God who sends his people to be a blessing to all of humankind. There is a human side of mission that is perceived in the movement of people, in the collection of funds, in the development of missionary organizations, in the planting and growing of new churches crossing geographical or sociological borders. But mission begins in the heart of God, and it is his initiative to which we humans respond. If Christian mission is first and foremost God's mission, Christians must always conduct mission in an attitude of humility and dependence on God. When the human dimensions of the missionary task overtake and determine the way in which mission is conducted, mission becomes a human activity without redemptive power. The paradoxes Paul describes in his letters to the Corinthians are evidence of a basic attitude, a spirituality nourished by a perception of the greatness of God's purpose and the sense of awe, privilege, worship, fear and trembling in human hearts sensitive to it.

The message that the missionaries have for the world is a message from God, who sends his messengers to let the earth hear his voice. The good news that the messengers bring is that God, who created this universe, loves his creation and calls his creatures to be reconciled to him.

It is true that the gospel is the good news about Jesus Christ and that apart from Jesus Christ there is no gospel. But what did Jesus himself teach? What was the theme of his preaching, and how did he explain his presence? Take the Sermon on the Mount—for many, the great summary of Jesus' teaching. Every line is about God, who Jesus constantly refers to as "Father." Or take the parables, which through a variety of images and metaphors have one main theme, the kingdom of God. And in pivotal moments of his ministry when he affirms his identity, it is always in reference to God. I am always deeply moved by Luke's narrative that describes a joyful Jesus receiving a report from his missionaries:

> At that same hour Jesus rejoiced in the Holy Spirit and said, "I thank you, Father, Lord of heaven and earth, because you have hidden these things from the wise and the intelligent and have revealed them to infants. . . . All things have been handed over to me by my Father; and no one knows who the Son is except the Father, or who the Father is except the Son and anyone to whom the Son chooses to reveal him." (Lk 10:21-22 NRSV)

In these words of Jesus we see how a profound sense of mission is grounded in the assurance of a relationship with God as loving Father, and that such assurance comes with joy from the Holy Spirit. This is one of those passages of the Gospels that has both a missionary as well as a trinitarian thrust, because the biblical foundation of mission is trinitarian, which explains why great moments of missionary advance are born in the cradle of spiritual revival. When, by a special visitation of the Holy Spirit, Christians have a renewed sense of the majesty, power and love of God, the grace and compassion of Jesus Christ, and the renewing fire of the Holy Spirit, the outcome is the renewal of missionary vocation. Churches that experience spiritual vitality are able to assess the world and its missionary needs, to discern the missionary thrust of Christian truth and to create the structures that will allow mission to happen. Pentecost is the first instance of such an event, and it is important to notice that during the twentieth century the strongest and most successful missionary action has come from the Pentecostal movement. For Pentecostals the experience described in Acts 2 is a foundational experience, a paradigm of how God continues to act in renewing his church and driving it to mission.

However, one does not need to be a Pentecostal to recognize this paradigm of God's accomplishment of his purpose in history. Valdir Steuernagel, a Brazilian Lutheran missiologist, shows in his book about models of missionary obedience how that principle worked in the early church, in the Franciscan movement and in the Moravian experience that was the cradle of Protestant missions. Howard Snyder, a Free Methodist missiologist, has written several books pointing to the same principle, especially as it was operative in the Methodist movement that was a missionary response to the needs of Britain at the beginning of the Industrial Revolution. Moravians and Methodists were spiritually alive people, and their spirituality nourished their missionary vision and action. Their influence flowed over to other sectors of Protestantism and was instrumental in the development of the world missionary movement that dominated the scene from the middle of the eighteenth to the twentieth century. Expressing the vision of a global evangelical fellowship, the Lausanne movement placed itself within that evangelical spirit in which awareness of God's missionary purpose leads to an attitude of worship and a commitment to obey:

> We affirm our belief in the one eternal God, Creator and Lord of the world, Father, Son and Holy Spirit, who governs all things according to the purpose of his will. He has been calling out from the world a people for himself and sending his people back into the world to be his servants and his witnesses, for the extension of his kingdom, the building up of Christ's body and the glory of his name. We confess with shame that we often denied our calling and failed in our mission by becoming conformed to the world or by withdrawing from it. Yet we rejoice that even when borne by earthen vessels, the Gospel is still a precious treasure. To the task of making that treasure known in the power of the Holy Spirit we desire to dedicate ourselves anew. (Lausanne Covenant, par. 1)

Christ: God's Best Missionary

HE WAS THE SON OF A RICH FAMILY, a delicate Japanese poet who by the middle of the twentieth century had become famous in his country as a pacifist and leader of social reform. As a young man, Toyohiko Kagawa's imagination was fired by the story of the young carpenter Jesus of Nazareth, and he became an ardent disciple whose vocation of service took him to be a missionary in the miserable slum district of Shinkawa, Kobe. Serving the poor, preaching, writing poems and going to jail for his convictions at a time when his country was geared to wage war, Kagawa became a symbol of Christianity in his country.

Around the same time, a young revolutionary schoolteacher in Mexico decided to take seriously the evangelical faith that his adoptive father had taught him as a child. He became a follower of Jesus, working as a missionary teacher in the primary school of a remote village. Gonzalo Baez-Camargo taught and wrote, studied theology and became a Bible translator, and thousands of Mexicans read his contemporary version of the Jesus story from his weekly columns in *Excelsior*, the newspaper with the largest circulation in his country.

A few years later a young woman born in Yugoslavia into an Albanian peasant family consecrated her life to Jesus, became a nun and went as a missionary to India. After seventeen years as a teacher, Mother Teresa felt called to serve the poorest of the poor, adopted Indian dress and nationality, and founded the Missionary of Charity Order. Her service to children, lepers and the beggars dying in the streets made an impact around the world, and a growing number of young people followed her. In 1979 she received the Nobel Peace Prize.

Men and women such as these were captivated by Jesus; they followed him on the road of sacrificial service and left a unique mark on the history of twentieth-century Christianity. Their lives and writings continue to inspire new generations of Christians.

JESUS, THE GOOD NEWS OF THE GOSPEL

One might summarize the history of Christian mission as the way in which people in thousands of cultures and languages have come to know Jesus, the way in which the name of Jesus has been proclaimed and honored from country to country, from culture to culture, from language to language, from century to century. In the history of humankind Jesus has inspired artists to write books, paint pictures and compose music in such a way that the memory of millions of human beings today from all races, cultures and religions has a place for Jesus. There is an element of mystery in the way in which Jesus of Nazareth continues to attract people, to capture the hearts and minds of an amazing variety of people in an amazing variety of places. As a testimony of Jesus' power to influence people, consider the fact that the way we date events relates to his coming into our world and our history. As I write this I am living more than two thousand years after Jesus' birth, and most people around the world will acknowledge that fact and thus testify to the impact of the carpenter from Nazareth on the history of humankind.

At precisely the right time in history, writes the apostle Paul (Gal 4:4), Jesus came to earth. Jesus taught that the Father had sent him, and John's Gospel stresses that this sending of Jesus was an expression of God's love for humankind. Thus the heart of the Gospel is encapsulated

in the famous verse that Luther considered to be the gospel in minia-
ture: "God so loved the world that he gave his only Son" (Jn 3:16 NRSV).
The priestly prayer of Jesus for his disciples (Jn 17) is permeated by a
clear awareness of his own *being sent* as much as by his own *sending* of
his disciples to be missionaries in the world. Jesus was sent by God the
Father and was God's best missionary, the true model for Christian mission. Jesus is the Christ, the "anointed one" whom the missionary God
promised as his missionary par excellence, the "Messiah" whom the
people of the Bible expected. This is why we have come to know him
as Jesus "Christ."

Jesus the missionary continues to inspire people in a unique way to
become missionaries. Among different cultures and peoples the impact
of the life of Jesus continues to inspire acts of courage as service to God
and other people. In his dialogue with a Hindu interlocutor on religions,
Indian writer Vishal Mangalwadi reminds us that "missionaries have
gone to remote, hostile and dangerous parts of the world and won over
their enemies." He asks why there is no similar volunteerism among
Hindu youth: "Why doesn't Hindu nationalism breed volunteerism that
struggles against moral and physical suffering? Why are ninety-seven
percent of the volunteers with Mother Teresa foreigners?" His own response is both eloquent and forceful: "Knowing, loving and serving a
transcendent and personal God is at the root of all western volunteerism.
Missionaries are usually the most heroic expression of that volunteerism
because they give their whole lives to it."[1] The writer himself is a missionary among his own people in India.

Jesus continues to inspire people because his story is continually
transmitted through preaching, Bible distribution, film, video, music
and several forms of art. This transmission of the Jesus story is at the center of missionary activity. One of the first tasks of evangelical missionary
work among people who have never heard the gospel is to translate one
of the Gospels into the language of those people. This is in line with the
earliest Christian mission work. Proclaiming the story of Jesus was the

thrust of the apostolic preaching after Pentecost to both Jewish audiences (Acts 4:8-12) and Gentile inquirers (Acts 10:34-43). Jesus Christ was also the core of the apostolic letters to the young churches sprouting up in the first century (1 Jn 1:1-4), and the preaching and teaching of the apostle Paul (1 Cor 15:1-8). As Paul said about his own missionary practice, the apostles did not preach themselves but Jesus Christ (1 Cor 2:1-2). Peter emphasized that their message was not literary fiction or an invention but a testimony of what they had experienced with Christ (2 Pet 1:16-21). Only in Christ is there salvation.

The fourth paragraph of the Lausanne Covenant provides a helpful summary of the gospel and the nature of evangelism: "To evangelize is to spread the good news that Jesus Christ died for our sins and was raised from the dead according to the Scriptures, and that as the reigning Lord he now offers the forgiveness of sins and the liberating gift of the Spirit to all who repent and believe."

The Manila Manifesto of 1989 summarizes the gospel in the section "Good News for Today." This summary expresses well much of the evangelical missionary practice and reflection on the gospel on a global level that took place in the fifteen years following the issuing of the Lausanne Covenant:

We rejoice that the living God did not abandon us to our lostness and despair. In his love he came after us in Jesus Christ to rescue and remake us. So the good news focuses on the historic person of Jesus, who came proclaiming the Kingdom of God and living a life of humble service, who died for us, becoming sin and curse in our place, and whom God vindicated by raising him from the dead. To those who repent and believe in Christ, God grants a share in the new creation. He gives us new life, which includes the forgiveness of our sins and the indwelling transforming power of his Spirit. He welcomes us into his new community, which consists of people of all races, nations and cultures. And he promises that one day we will enter his new world, in which evil will be abolished, nature will be redeemed and God will reign for ever.[2]

At least four elements in this statement are important from the perspective of Christian mission. The first is the reference to the historic fact of Jesus, his teaching and his lifestyle. The second is the reference to his death and resurrection, and their meaning for all human beings. The third is the reference to the personal response required from those who hear the good news about Jesus. The fourth is the reference to the consequences that follow for those who respond to the good news.

In relation to the first element, Jesus continues to inspire people all over the world. Even in the middle of the cultural changes to which I have referred in previous chapters, the person of our Lord continues to captivate minds and imaginations. The scenes of Jesus' life and his stories and sayings in the four Gospels attract thousands of readers. For instance, at the Cairo Book Fair, the second most important book fair in the world, the Gospels are among the bestsellers and especially attract young people. Jesus also continues to inspire great writers such as the Portuguese Nobel Prize winner José Saramago. Vinoth Ramachandra from Sri Lanka calls our attention to how Jesus is perceived in feminist critique of the traditional male dominance in many cultures: "Many women see in him a man who was liberated from the pervasive chauvinism of his society, at ease in the company of women. He showed them respect not only by teaching them and inviting them to minister to him, but by often associating with the most despised among them, so risking his reputation as a prophet-rabbi."[3] I felt embarrassed some years ago when a simple housewife from the church on whose pastoral team I was serving confronted me with the weight of these facts. They are there, recorded in the Gospels, but churches in many places have lost the memory of them, perhaps because of a reluctance to act on the principles that follow from considering the example of Jesus.

As I consider questions posed by a postmodern culture, my own evangelistic experience of decades of communicating the gospel to young people leads me to agree with Howard Snyder that, after all, Jesus may fit postmodern sensibilities better than he does modern or premodern views. In a book about postmodernity in Latin America, I challenged my readers to consider that frequently our evangelical preaching and teaching has made Jesus look more like a disciplinarian schoolteacher or a solemn professor of systematic theology than the kind of open-air peasant storyteller that he was. Snyder summarizes the question well: "The modern worldview in its various forms remade Jesus in its own image—philosopher, poet, philanthropist or lawgiver. Postmodernism helpfully shatters these earlier worldviews, just possibly making Jesus accessible and understandable as never before."[4] Yes, *the historic person of Jesus,* who came proclaiming the kingdom of God and living a life of humble service, continues to attract all kinds of people in all kinds of cultures.

It is in relation to the second and third elements of the statement quoted above that more controversial questions come: Jesus died for us, becoming sin and a curse in our place; God vindicated him by raising him from the dead; and as a consequence, to those who repent and believe in Christ, God grants a share in the new creation. Many confessed admirers of Jesus find it difficult to believe that the death of this wonderful, attractive preacher and prophet may have something to do with our own need to repent from sins and to accept God's gift of eternal life. It is what the apostle Paul called the scandal of the cross (1 Cor 1:23). And many people consider it an unacceptable imposition that because of the resurrection of Jesus Christ he is entitled to be the Lord of our life, so that we have to renounce any other master, be it intellectual pride, love of pleasure, lust for power, racial prejudice or spiritual superiority. Even people who have grown up in a Christianized society or family sometimes find it difficult to come to terms with their personal need for a Savior and Lord.

Consider one of Jesus' short statements about his person and vocation: "The Son of Man did not come to be served, but to serve, and to give his life as a ransom for many" (Mt 20:28). Many admirers and even imitators of Jesus' attitude of service reject the idea that they need to be redeemed from slavery to sin and condemnation. John Stott is the theologian who has best expounded this aspect of the gospel:

What the gospel announces, according to the New Testament, is not just what Christ offers people today, but what he once did to make this offer possible. The apostolic gospel brings together the past and the present, the once and the now, historical event and contemporary experience. It declares not only that Jesus saves, but that he died for our sins, and was raised from death in order to be able to do so. The gospel is not preached if the saving power is proclaimed and the saving events omitted, especially the cross.[5]

The fourth element of the Manila Manifesto has to do with God's gifts for those who accept his way of salvation through Jesus Christ. These are given, as a motivation for joyful and enthusiastic Christian living, to believers who accept the privilege of becoming involved in what Father, Son and Holy Spirit are doing in the world. In Latin America thousands have come to know Jesus as Savior and Lord because they first experienced the gift of acceptance in a local church and belonging to a new family. But I also know many who refuse to follow Jesus because that would mean accepting as brothers and sisters people from the lower social classes, or sharing with the poor the material blessings they enjoy. Others have not yet experienced the abundant life into which they have been called because they have become used to living their church life as a formal weekly routine in which there is no engagement with the real issues of life. Christian discipleship and spiritual growth have to do with the unfolding of God's loving purpose for each of us, including our participation in his mission.

CONVERSION TO CHRIST

Most Protestant missionary activity during the nineteenth and twentieth centuries came from the Christ-centered evangelical movements we associate with Pietism and the Moravians in central Europe, and the revivals in the English-speaking world. The good news that evangelical missionaries proclaimed was centered in the person and work of Jesus Christ. Theologian Alister McGrath reminds us that the evangelical stance is radically Christ-centered. As a consequence, evangelical mission was also Christ-centered. McGrath relates this to the high view of Scripture to which evangelicals are committed: "Christology and scriptural authority are inextricably linked, in that it is Scripture, and Scripture alone that brings us to the true and saving knowledge of Jesus Christ."[6]

One important aspect of the Christ-focused evangelical conviction that has shaped evangelical mission is a clear call to obedience and commitment, because what God has done for human beings in Christ demands a faith response. It is an emphasis that distinguishes evangelicals from others. In the 1980s there was sustained dialogue between evangelicals and Roman Catholics about mission, in which the participants discovered much common ground.[7] However, in the section on the biblical basis of mission, the report of this dialogue shows evidence of a certain tension: "While both sides affirm that the pilgrim church is missionary by its very nature, its missionary activity is differently understood." It goes on to explain the Catholic position following the Vatican II definition of the church as "sacrament of salvation . . . *the sign and promise of redemption to each and every person without exception*." It then states that most evangelicals have a contrasting position:

> The Church is the beginning and anticipation of the new creation, the first born among his creatures. Though in Adam all die, *not all are automatically in Christ*. So life in Christ has to be received by grace with repentance, through faith. *With yearning Evangelicals plead for a response to the atoning work of Christ in his death and resurrection*. But with sorrow they know that not all who are called are chosen.

This conviction is then reflected in missionary activity: "Evangelization is therefore *the call to those outside to come* as children of the Father into the fullness of eternal life in Christ by the Spirit, and into the joy of a loving community in the fellowship of the Church."[8]

This call to conversion is crucial for evangelical mission. Personal encounter with Jesus Christ changes people. Sometimes it is a radical change, and there is a component of moral transformation in this concept of conversion. One could say that in much evangelical missionary practice there has been a certain tension. On the one hand there is pessimism about human nature derived from the biblical teaching about human beings recovered by the Reformation, in contrast to the Catholic idea that human beings can work out their own salvation or achieve merits toward it. Wesley, Pietists and other evangelical leaders retained this Reformation perspective and were also skeptical of the growing optimism, rooted in the Enlightenment, about human ability to build a perfect social order. But there was also an optimism about God's grace and its regenerating and transforming power that became a mark of evangelical missionary and evangelistic efforts. This tension or balance is also evident, for instance, in Pentecostal evangelism in Latin America, which rejects the practices of popular religion to appease God or gain his favor, while accepting with enthusiasm the transforming power of the gospel. Human religious practices have no power to give salvation to human beings, but there is power in the blood of Jesus Christ to regenerate people by the power of the Holy Spirit.

Evangelical missionaries in countries that are nominally Christian or where other religions are dominant have been criticized for their emphasis on conversion. Muslims in Africa, like Roman Catholics in Latin America, accuse evangelicals of working against the cultural integrity of people when they call them to conversion. A joint group from the World Evangelical Fellowship and the Lausanne Committee that convened to consider this issue in 1988 concluded by issuing the "Hong Kong Call to Conversion," which states clearly:

> Conversion means turning from sin in repentance to Christ in faith. Through this faith believers are forgiven and justified and adopted into the family of God's children and heirs. In the turning process, they are invited to the crucified and risen Christ by the Holy Spirit who prompts them to die to the sinful desires of their old nature and to be liberated from Satanic bondage and to become new creatures in Him. This is their

passage from spiritual death to spiritual life, which Scripture calls regeneration or new birth (Jn 3:5).[9]

Because mission frequently involves transcultural action, it is important to be alert to forms of evangelism and conversion that appear to involve the imposition of foreign cultural patterns on the receptors of the gospel. The Lausanne Covenant contained a warning, reminding us that "missions have all too frequently exported with the gospel an alien culture, and churches have sometimes been in bondage to culture rather than to Scripture" (par. 10). The "Hong Kong Call" offers a more specific reminder that "there is a radical discontinuity in all conversions, in the sense that the convert 'turns from darkness to light and from the power of Satan to God' (Acts 26:18)." However, it also strives to make clear that "conversion should not 'deculturize' the converts. They should remain members of their cultural community, and wherever possible retain the values that are not contrary to biblical revelation. In no case should the converts be forced to be 'converted' to the culture of the foreign missionary."[10]

A CHRISTOLOGICAL PATTERN FOR MISSION

If Christ is at the center of the gospel and of missionary activity, his way of being God's missionary also becomes a pattern for life and mission. René Padilla has expressed well an evangelical perspective recovered from a fresh reading of the Gospels: "Jesus Christ is God's missionary *par excellence*, and he involves his followers in his mission."[11] As we find it in the Gospels, Jesus' mission includes *fishing for the kingdom*, or, in other words, the call to conversion to Jesus Christ, who is the way, the truth and the life. Conversion to Jesus stands as the foundation on which the Christian community is built.

Mission also includes *compassion* as a result of deep involvement with the multitudes and their needs. It is neither a sentimental burst of emotion nor an academic option for the poor, but definite and intentional actions of service in order to feed the multitude with bread *for* life, as well as a sharing of the Bread *of* life. Mission includes *confrontation* between the powers of death and the power of the Suffering Servant; thus suffering becomes a mark of Jesus' messianic mission and a result of this power struggle, and of human injustice. Through creative contextual obedience Jesus' mission becomes a fertile source of inspiration, because it contains the seeds of new patterns being explored today through practice and reflection, patterns involving a simple lifestyle, holistic mission, the unity of the church for mission, God's kingdom as missiological paradigm and spiritual conflict in mission.

In Christ's incarnation, crucifixion and resurrection is a pattern that shapes mission done in the name of Christ. The christological paradigm of mission found in the Gospels is incarnational: "The Word became flesh and made his dwelling among us" (Jn 1:14). Jesus' mission was accomplished within the limited realities of a given time and space. As we confess in the Creed, he suffered under Pontius Pilate, a statement that involves a date and a geographical place. John Stott reminds us that "the Son of God did not stay in the safe immunity of his heaven, remote from human sin and tragedy. He actually entered our world. He emptied himself of his glory and humbled himself to serve."[12] The witness of the Gospels allows us to see the humanity of Jesus Christ, the social structure and the economic realities within which he lived, taught and ministered. Only with due regard to these can we begin to understand the content and direction of his teaching. Why would God choose to have Jesus born among animals, in a manger? Why would Jesus call as his disciples people as disparate as the tax collector Levi and the guerrilla fighter Simon the Zealot? Why would Jesus tell stories in which the heroes were Samaritans?

If Jesus' incarnational pattern is taken seriously by missionaries today within the social and structural realities of our time and space, mission will not be done from a platform of power and privilege, nor will the gospel be watered down to make it palatable to the rich and powerful. Again John Stott puts it well:

Now [Jesus] sends us into the world, as the Father sent him into the world (John 17:18; 20:21). In other words our mission is to be modeled on his. Indeed all authentic mission is incarnational mission. It demands identification without loss of identity. It means entering other people's worlds as he entered ours, though without compromising our Christian convictions, values or standards.[13]

Viv Grigg is a New Zealander who went as a missionary to the Philippines. At first he lived in a middle-class section of Manila where most of the Western missionaries live. One day, inspired by the Gospels and also by the stories of Francis of Assisi and Toyohiko Kagawa, he moved to Tatalon, one of the most depressed areas of the city. Grigg's experience of incarnation among the poor opened for him a world of biblical understanding he had not seen before. I use his book *Companion to the Poor*[14] as a textbook, and my students of all nationalities always find him challenging and enlightening.

Jesus' mission was marked by the cross, which also points toward a clearly defined spirit of sacrificial service: "The Son of Man did not come to be served, but to serve, and to give his life as a ransom for many" (Mt 20:28). This statement is matched by the many accounts in the Gospels in which we see Jesus serving those in need and showing the ultimate example of a humble, sacrificial lifestyle. We recall from the pages of the Gospels the stories of Jesus healing lepers by touching them, paying attention to a blind man along the road, taking time to hold children and bless them, teaching the hungry crowds patiently, and washing his disciples' feet on the eve of his Passion. Undoubtedly the Evangelists chose these stories to communicate how Jesus' actions matched his words about a spirit of service. The roots of the servant approach are in the message of the prophet Isaiah about the Suffering Servant, and we see them developed in the theological elaboration of the Christology of Paul, Peter, John and other apostolic writers.

This reference to a missionary style marked by the cross has come to be understood as a corrective to all forms of triumphalism, and consequently it is taken seriously by evangelicals around the world.[15] The shift of attention to the Johannine version of the Great Commission led to a new appreciation of the humanity of Jesus Christ and the importance of his incarnational style of mission. This was a fertile source for evaluation and self-criticism within the evangelical missionary enterprise. One finds it as a theme in the Lausanne Covenant and as a hermeneutical key in several documents produced later by the Lausanne movement and the World Evangelical Fellowship.

A classic aspect of Christian spirituality, the imitation of Christ, or *imitatio Christi*, has now taken a missiological dimension. In the context of social and political tensions in places such as South Africa and Latin America, and in the world of ethnic minorities in the United States, the imitation of Christ was connected with suffering and martyrdom for the sake of the gospel. We are in debt to some forms of liberation theology for reminding us that the Gospel narratives about the Passion and death of Jesus have the sociopolitical dimensions of Jesus' prophetic ministry. Jesus' fierce criticism of the hypocrisy of religious and political leaders such as the Pharisees and of the business conducted by the Sadducees in the Jerusalem temple was ministry with political connotations. Jesus was condemned to death because he became dangerous to the religious and political establishment. Many missionaries in recent history have been killed, tortured or imprisoned because they also became politically dangerous, even though their motivation was none other than serving the poor in a spirit of imitation of Christ. Jesus referred to this self-sacrificial dimension of mission when he taught us that "unless a grain of wheat falls into the earth and dies, it remains just a single grain; but if it dies, it bears much fruit" (Jn 12:24 NRSV). He was talking about himself but also warning us about the cost of discipleship.

For evangelicals, however, it is clear that biblical Christology includes an unequivocal reference to the atoning work of Jesus Christ on the cross and the need of every person to respond to it. In this respect the death of Christ is unique; no other death can ever equal it. As we have seen, this truth is central to the gospel. As a consequence, there cannot be an imitation of Christ in the biblical sense without a new birth. René Padilla, in his commentary on the liberation Christology of Jesuit theologian Jon Sobrino, accepts the truth, based on examination of the texts of the Gospels, that the death of Jesus was the historical outcome of the kind of life he lived, and that he suffered for the cause of justice and challenges us to do the same. But Padilla also warns us to remember that "unless the death of Christ is also seen as God's gracious provision of an atonement for sin, the basis for forgiveness is removed and sinners are left without the hope of justification. . . . Salvation is by grace through faith and . . . nothing should detract from the generosity of God's mercy and love as the basis of joyful obedience to the Lord Jesus Christ."[16]

Mission according to Jesus' pattern is also mission carried on in the power of the resurrection, by the gift of the Holy Spirit. In all four versions of the Great Commission it is the resurrected Christ who sends the disciples on their mission. The authority that is the basis for the activity of the missionary is the authority of the Lord Jesus Christ, who said, "All authority in heaven and on earth has been given to me. Therefore go" (Mt 28:18-19). The apostle Paul developed this truth about the nature of the power and authority of the missionary in 2 Corinthians, in which there are numerous references to his own missionary style as well as theological statements about its christological basis (e.g., 2 Cor 3:1-6; 4:5-14; 10:1-6). This is in open contrast to the missionary style and method that developed later in Christian history. At the worst point of Constantinian mission the authority of the missionaries was perceived as coming from the kings and queens of conquering nations and so came to be based, as we have seen, on military, economic or technological power rather than on the power of the resurrection.

As we consider the missionary pattern modeled by Jesus and the meaning of his death and resurrection, we also come to face the uniqueness of his person and work, which we must acknowledge is a scandalous truth, a puzzling reality. We see in the Gospel stories that it was surprising for his contemporaries, and it continues to be a challenge to human logic in these times of religious pluralism. Sri Lankan theologian Vinoth Ramachandra has posed the question forcefully:

> Along with the unassuming and meek posture Jesus demonstrates in his relationships with other people, there are also the extraordinary and startling claims he makes, both implicitly and explicitly, concerning his person and vocation; it is these that eventually prompt the progression from puzzlement to hostility and to outright rage.[17]

Ramachandra reminds us of Jesus' claims to enjoy a unique filial relationship with God, to be the unique fulfillment of Jewish Scripture and to be in a different category from others. This uniqueness is part and parcel of the gospel we proclaim, and, as Ramachandra very ably demonstrates in his book, it is truth consistent with the logic of the gospel story. It may sound arrogant to people who follow other masters and traditions, and we must acknowledge that sometimes missionaries have proclaimed it with an arrogance that came from cultural superiority. However, it is this uniqueness that makes Jesus Lord of all and the Lord of mission.

The christological pattern for mission we have discussed here arises from the heart of the gospel, the completed work of Jesus Christ, who is God's final revelation to human beings and God's missionary par excellence. This pattern becomes especially relevant as we enter an era in which young churches will make a significant contribution to global mission. In most cases these churches lack political, social or economic power. As in the first century of our era, the only power the missionaries will have is the power of the Spirit, who takes them to the ends of the world, and the power of the resurrected Christ, who assures them of a final victory beyond the hardships and struggles of the present.

7

The Holy Spirit and Christian Mission

BISHOP JOHN V. TAYLOR OPENS HIS BOOK *The Go-Between God,* one of the most creative and challenging studies on the Holy Spirit and Christian mission that I know, with the following paragraphs:

> The chief actor in the historic mission of the Christian church is the Holy Spirit. He is the director of the whole enterprise. The mission consists of things that he is doing in the world. In a special way it consists of the light that he is focusing upon Jesus Christ.
>
> This fact, so patent to Christians in the first century, is largely forgotten in our own. So we have lost our nerve and our sense of direction and have turned the divine initiative into a human enterprise. "It all depends on me" is an attitude that is bedeviling both the practice and the theology of our mission in these days.[1]

Bishop Taylor was a missionary in Africa and later the general secretary of the Church Missionary Society. His work confirms my conviction that when missionaries reflect on their experience they become the best theologians. Their theology is lively because it connects with the daily life of the church at the frontiers of missionary action.

When I read Bishop Taylor's words to a Pentecostal Bible school teacher in Canada, where I was working at the time the book was published, he shouted "Hallelujah! . . . That is exactly what we Pentecostals have always believed." Then with a mischievous smile he added, "But it is great to see that Anglicans are coming to agree with us!" Though said in a humorous manner, the observation in a way summarized what has taken place in mission theology during the twentieth century. The astounding growth of the Pentecostal movement around the world has brought to the forefront of theological reflection important questions about the Holy Spirit that have been central to missiological reflection and writing in recent years. This happened partly because Pentecostals put great emphasis on the presence and power of the Holy Spirit but also because theologians and Bible scholars interested in the mission of the church rediscovered the important role the Holy Spirit plays in not only the Pauline epistles but also the Gospels, especially Luke-Acts. The missionary facts of the twentieth century, such as the shift of Christianity southward and the end of Christendom, have brought the rediscovery of the Bible as a missionary book.

PENTECOSTAL GROWTH

Measuring the growth of churches is a complex task, and whenever figures are quoted the tentative nature of these statistics has to be kept in mind. David Barrett is considered to be one of the best-informed specialists in statistics about Christianity. In his article for the *Dictionary of Pentecostal and Charismatic Movements* he estimated that by 1988 there were 332 million affiliated Pentecostals. In this figure he included members of classic Pentecostal churches and charismatics within non-Pentecostal churches. From this total, 71 percent were nonwhite, 66 percent lived in the Third World, 87 percent lived in poverty, and the majority were urban settlers.[2]

Another scholar who has specialized in the study of Pentecostal movements around the world is Walter Hollenweger, a Pentecostal himself from Switzerland. He writes about three streams: the *classic Pentecos-*

tal churches, the *charismatic movements* within traditional churches and the emergent *indigenous nonwhite churches*. Though Hollenweger places all three within Pentecostalism, his reference to indigenous nonwhite churches is important because many of these developed in Africa, Asia and Latin America without any connection to a classic Pentecostal denomination or mission. Local initiatives and contexts are to be taken into account to avoid the use of *Pentecostal* as a Western blanket term that does not do justice to reality. The African-Initiated Churches, for instance, have some characteristics similar to Pentecostal churches but have unique distinctives that fit them into a category of their own.

Most of the churches within classic Pentecostalism trace their origin to the movement that developed at the beginning of the twentieth century in North America. This stream sprang from sources in humble places, such as the charismatic experience of a woman in Topeka, Kansas, at a Bible school in 1901, under the influence of Charles Parham; or the ministry of William Seymour, a black preacher in an old building at Azusa Street in Los Angeles in 1906. Pentecostal missiologist Gary McGee says of this initial generation that they believed apostolic "signs and wonders" that had characterized the advance of the early Christians in the book of Acts had been restored:

> Traditional Pentecostalism distinguishes between the work of the Spirit in regeneration and his work in empowering believers for ministry. When one has received this empowerment it is referred to as the baptism of the Spirit. This person knows that she/he has received this baptism if, at that time, she/he spoke in tongues. Speaking in tongues is called "the initial evidence."[3]

Thus in Pentecostal churches people experience glossolalia (speaking in tongues) or special revelations of God through dreams and visions, and healing through prayer and imposition of hands. All these foster a great boldness in evangelization and are attributed to a special and unique action of the Holy Spirit, who fills a person. Thus the Pentecostal movement is seen as a restoration of the apostolic faith of the first century.

Sociological observation points out that the numerical growth of Pentecostals takes place especially among socially marginalized groups that suffer uprooting and anomie during periods of rapid urbanization. Also, some aspects of Pentecostal religious life and theological emphasis coincide with characteristics of the culture of poverty, such as an oral liturgy, narrative theology, uninhibited emotionalism, maximum participation in prayer and worship, dreams and visions, and an intense search for community and belonging. These traits are also characteristic of the popular nonwhite churches. On the other hand, after more than a century of existence and a process of institutionalization, several old Pentecostal churches are now middle or upper middle class in composition, thanks to the social mobility made possible by conversion experiences that brought a reorientation of life and new social and economic habits, followed by progress in the following generation.

Sociological considerations aside, when we explore the origins of the Pentecostal movement we see a variety of sources and patterns such as the Holiness movement in the second part of the nineteenth century, charismatic experiences among missionaries who wanted to be more effective and fruitful, or protests of young indigenous churches that felt constrained by rigid foreign missionary policies. Missionary concern and passion as well as a search for a deeper spiritual life seem to be common denominators in most cases. I can think of one case that illustrates the point. In 1906 Minnie F. Abrams, who had been an American missionary of the Methodist church in India since 1897, read about the Welsh revival. She and the Indian women among whom she worked in the Mukti Mission experienced what she described as a baptism of the Holy Spirit. She wrote a book describing the revival, *The Baptism of the Holy Ghost and Fire*, in which she discussed its theological underpinnings. She sent a copy to May Hoover, the wife of Willis Hoover, a medical doctor who was also a Methodist missionary in Valparaiso, Chile. The Hoovers and several Chilean believers also had an experience like the one described by Minnie Abrams. The search for a deeper spiritual life took some to excesses, but the reaction against them paralyzed the more conservative Methodists. In contrast to Hoover, his missionary colleagues hardened their attitudes and were not always sensitive to concerns of Chilean believers. By 1911 Hoover and several followers had left the Methodist church and founded the Pentecostal Methodist Church, today the largest denomination in Chile.[4]

MISSIOLOGICAL EXPLORATIONS

Pentecostal missiologists agree that though there has been a great deal of Pentecostal missionary activity on a global scale since the earliest stages of the movement, there has been no theological reflection on it. One interesting example, which may be the first effort to systematize the missiological principles followed by classic Pentecostals, was the work of Melvin Hodges, an Assemblies of God missionary in El Salvador from 1935 to 1945 and later a mission executive until 1985. Before going as a missionary Hodges had studied the works of Roland Allen, and once in the field he applied them to redirect missionary methods "from a paternalistic structure dependent upon American financial assistance to one based on indigenous church principles."[5] Hodges's work is a reflection on his own experience in a part of the world where churches had grown at an impressive rate, but he also expounded the principles for an indigenous approach to mission developed in Allen's classic books *Missionary Methods: St. Paul's or Ours* (1912) and *The Spontaneous Expansion of the Church and the Causes That Hinder It* (1927). Allen, who had been an Anglican missionary in China from 1895 to 1902, became highly critical of the missionary methodology predominant at his time. In his books he advocated a radical return to New Testament patterns of mission.

Some of the areas of mission studies that Allen pursued were the role of laypersons in the missionary work of the church, the need for flexible ministry patterns and realistic financial policies. Allen became convinced that the paid ministry, as it was conceived in sending countries like England, should not be exported to mission territories, because the same pattern could not be reproduced in a different context. The pattern also hindered the participation of laypersons in ministry. The missionary practice of using foreign funds from the mission to pay national pastors created dependency. Allen's study of the New Testament convinced him that the Western church had departed too far from the biblical models. The beginning of the Pentecostal movement brought lay participation in evangelism, unpaid ministry, and contextual forms of worship and evangelism among the poor. Allen also stressed the cruciality of the presence and power of the Holy Spirit for mission and wrote extensively about it.[6] Though Allen did not know the Pentecostal movement, the coincidences are evident, which explains why a Pentecostal missiologist like Hodges would be an enthusiast for Allen's ideas.

In this way the missiological reflection of a High Anglican connected with the practice of a Pentecostal, and "Hodges, in fact, pentecostalized Allen's principles and rephrased them for his tradition."[7] When one reads Allen's book *Pentecost and the World: The Revelation of the Holy Spirit in the Acts of the Apostles* (1917), it is not difficult to understand why his work would resonate in the heart of a Pentecostal. Besides Allen's principles, Hodges also adopted as basic for his own theology of mission classic tenets of the evangelical position, such as the authority of the Scriptures, the centrality of Christ, the dynamics of the Holy Spirit, the lostness of humankind apart from saving grace and the importance of the church as God's instrument in evangelism. His work influenced the missionary policies of the Assemblies of God, but he did not reflect specifically about the uniqueness of the Pentecostal experience. From my observation in Latin America, North America and Europe I would say that Pentecostal and charismatic churches have kept closer than other denominations to the New Testament pattern explored by Allen.[8]

As some critics of Allen have pointed out, the New Testament principles he emphasized must be applied with the sociocultural context of apostolic times in mind, giving due regard to contemporary contexts.

Missiologists from other traditions were among the first to carry out careful research into questions about the role of the Holy Spirit in mission, trying to understand the kind of spontaneous expansion of the church characteristic of the Pentecostal movement. One of them was Lesslie Newbigin, who as early as 1953 wrote *The Household of God*, a book now considered a classic work on the nature and mission of the church. In this book Newbigin calls his readers to consider the importance of the Pentecostal movement from the perspective of church history. He describes Catholic ecclesiology, which emphasizes continuity with the apostles through St. Peter and Rome as the mark of the true church. Then he considers Protestant ecclesiology, which emphasizes the correct administration of the Word and the sacraments as the mark of the true church. Side by side with these long traditions he places the Pentecostal churches, with their emphasis on the presence and power of the Holy Spirit as the mark of the true church. Pointing to deadlocks in the ecumenical dialogues of the 1950s between Catholics and Protestants he wondered if

> the way forward may be found in a new understanding of the doctrine of the Holy Spirit. But of course that illumination which is needed will never come as a result of purely academic theological study. May it not be that the great Churches of the Catholic and the Protestant traditions will have to be humble enough to receive it in fellowship with their brethren in the various groups of the Pentecostal type with whom at present they have scarcely any fellowship at all?[9]

The understanding of the initiative of the Holy Spirit in relation to mission has been enriched by the contributions of several evangelical scholars. Their works provide a solid foundation for a better understanding of the evangelical practice of mission.[10] In his book *Pentecost and Missions* Harry Boer reminds us that the use of the Great Commission as the imperative motto for evangelical missionary work is a relatively recent development. The biblical pattern stresses the presence and power of the Holy Spirit in the life of the church as the source of missionary dynamism. Not a new legalism but the free, joyous expression of a renewed experience of God's grace provides a key to understand what may be the inspiration for the spontaneous missionary thrust in evangelical missions and churches around the world.

In his most recent writing about the ministry of the Holy Spirit, John Stott reminds us that in the twentieth century there was "an unfortunate disagreement among evangelical Christians about the work of the Holy Spirit." He thinks the tension comes from two points. While it is evident that "Pentecostalism is today the fastest growing Christian movement in the world, providing abundant evidence of God's blessing upon it," among some evangelicals "there is genuine anxiety that it is often growth without depth so that there is much superficiality everywhere." However, Stott has the conviction that "what unites evangelicals in our doctrine and experience of the Holy Spirit is considerably greater than what divides us."[11] His attitude of concentrating more on the agreements than on the disagreements is consonant with the consensus reached in Lausanne, expressed so well in the Covenant:

> We believe in the power of the Holy Spirit. The Father sent his Spirit to bear witness to his Son; without his witness ours is futile. Conviction of sin, faith in Christ, new birth and Christian growth are all his work. Further, the Holy Spirit is a missionary Spirit; thus evangelism should arise spontaneously from a Spirit-filled church. A church that is not a missionary church is contradicting itself and quenching the Spirit. World wide evangelization will become a realistic possibility only when the Spirit renews the church in truth and wisdom, faith, holiness, love and power. (par. 14)

THE HOLY SPIRIT AND MISSION

As we consider the biblical teaching about the power and direction of the Holy Spirit for Christian mission we ask questions prompted by our current missionary experience. Thus we come to realize how the missionary experience of the twentieth century has helped us to better understand the New Testament missionary patterns and, in relation to them, the teaching of Jesus Christ and the apostles about the Holy Spirit. In evangelical tradition the Pauline writings and John's Gospel have been the main sources of teaching about the Holy Spirit. In the second part of the twentieth century the teaching of Luke-Acts also became an important source. Roland Allen's work was a pioneer effort in this direction. All this is well expressed by evangelist and scholar Ajith Fernando from Sri Lanka: "The Charismatic movement has focused much attention on the abiding teachings that can come from Acts. . . . The result of this is that now we are looking more at the theology of Luke and therefore at the theology of the Holy Spirit. In this process the church seems to have recovered the missionary character of the Holy Spirit."[12]

I outline below points I regard as especially important for mission today.

1. *The word of promise becomes a reality by the work of the Spirit.* We find especially in Luke-Acts a pattern in which the missionary events are the fulfillment of what God's Word has promised or announced. When Jesus, "in the power of the Spirit," starts his ministry in the synagogue of Nazareth, he reads from the prophet Isaiah, rolls the scroll up and tells the people, "Today this scripture is fulfilled in your hearing" (Lk 4:14-21). The reality of this man, who in the power of the Spirit has come this day to Nazareth, is the visible, historical reality in which the word of the prophet becomes fulfilled. We find the same when, after Pentecost and the visitation of the Holy Spirit, Peter explains what has happened along the lines of Jesus of Nazareth: "This is what was spoken by the prophet Joel" (Acts 2:16). In other words, the reality of the church in mission can be understood only from the perspective of faith, as a result of God's Word becoming action in the world. That is its causality. We do face a historical, visible, social, empirical reality, but the people who are part of it explain their reality as a result of God's action.

Another key moment in the advance of the church in Acts is interpreted similarly. The conversion of Gentiles, which provokes an initial crisis in the young church and brings about the convocation of what is termed the "first great council" in Acts 15, culminates in James's speech (Acts 15:13-21). James says that what has taken place agrees with the words of the prophets, "as it is written." Thus the coming of Gentiles to faith in Jesus Christ and the fact that they receive the Holy Spirit is seen as a fulfillment of Amos's prophecy (vv. 16-18).

2. *The ministry of Jesus is possible by the power of the Holy Spirit.* Boer says that "intense messianic concentration is characteristic of the Spirit's work in the Gospels and the first chapter of Acts. The manifestations of the Spirit are there almost wholly centered in or around Jesus as though in preparation for a mighty dispersion."[13] Beginning with the birth of Jesus, his life and ministry are possible only by a creative and powerful action of the Spirit (Lk 1:35). Luke emphasizes that action of the Holy Spirit working in the midst of history, through the ministry of Jesus, in order to accomplish God's purpose. The Spirit descends on him at his baptism (Lk 3:22), and he returns from the Jordan "full of the Holy Spirit" (Lk 4:1). He is "led by the Spirit in the desert" for the battle against the tempter (Lk 4:1). In the story of the temptation, Jesus affirms his way of going about his mission in obedience to God rather than following the subtle temptation proposed by the enemy. He returns "in the power of the Spirit" (Lk 4:14) to begin his ministry in Galilee.

In the Gospel of John we find a verse that can be considered a commentary on the facts that Luke describes: "He whom God has sent speaks the words of God, for he gives the Spirit without measure" (Jn 3:34 NRSV). Once in the Gospel of Luke, in a lesson about prayer, Jesus teaches his disciples that God will respond generously to those who pray for the gift of the Spirit (Lk 11:13). Such a gift for making possible the mission of the church would come from the resurrected and glorified Lord at Pentecost, not earlier (Jn 7:39). Any claim to follow the pattern of Jesus in mission must take this fact seriously. Mission in Jesus' way is possible only in dependence on the Spirit. It is arrogant for missionaries to plan strategies based entirely on human logic and calculation if their

Savior and Lord could accomplish *his* mission only through the power of the Holy Spirit. Like Jesus in the desert, either the church as a community or individual missionaries are many times tempted to work toward accomplishments that might be impressive but are in fact acts of disobedience to God.

3. *God uses people filled with the power of the Holy Spirit.* Those able to recognize how God is working are people who could be described as insignificant from the human point of view, but their discernment of God's action comes from the fact that they are filled with the Spirit. I find especially significant the birth narrative of John, in which the Spirit is active, filling him, the predecessor of Jesus, the one who will prepare the way for Jesus' ministry in Israel, even before his birth (Lk 1:15). The same Spirit's power overshadows Mary and makes her conceive miraculously (Lk 1:35). When the young, pregnant Mary visits her pregnant cousin Elizabeth, the latter is filled with the Holy Spirit and recognizes God's action in Mary. Mary then becomes an inspired proclaimer, giving new strength and power to a song from the Old Testament (Lk 1:39-55). Zechariah the priest is filled with the Holy Spirit to prophesy about his prophet son (Lk 1:67-79).

One of the joys of pastoral and missionary work is to see how, in the daily life and mission of the church, the Spirit of God continues to fill simple people like the characters in this narrative, and how he accomplishes his purpose of blessing all of humankind through them. If the Spirit of God is in action, it is not only in spectacular ways according to methods prescribed in manuals but also in the daily actions of faithful service that make possible the life of the church and the continuation of its ministry, because God's Word of promise is being fulfilled today as well. This perspective allows us to appreciate other aspects of the work of the Spirit in the book of Acts. Administrative tasks to serve the material needs of God's people require people "full of the Spirit," like the seven who became a second tier of leadership in Jerusalem after a crisis of multicultural relations (Acts 6:3). The proclamation and defense of the gospel, and even the confrontation of the powerful with God's Word, requires people filled with the Spirit (Acts 4:8-10). A prompt response to the Spirit is required for the pioneer task of going into new territories and crossing old social barriers in order to share the gospel (Acts 8:26-29).

4. *Jesus teaches about the work of the Holy Spirit in mission.* In John's Gospel we find Jesus' clearest teaching on the ministry of the Holy Spirit. To begin with, he says that the Holy Spirit will be sent by the Father to be with the disciples in view of the physical absence of Jesus himself (Jn 14:16). The Spirit will both remind the disciples what Jesus has taught them (Jn 14:25-26) and lead them into all the truth that Jesus has been unable to teach them while with them (Jn 16:12-13). These promises apply in the first instance to the apostles who were with Jesus in the upper room and were fulfilled in the writing of the New Testament. But they also have a secondary reference to the Spirit's continuing teaching ministry, the aim of which is to glorify Christ by taking truth from Christ and declaring it to the disciples (Jn 16:14-15). The Spirit and the disciples testify on behalf of Christ. There is a connection between the testimony of the Spirit to the church and the testimony of the church to the world. The presence of the Spirit among the disciples in the church is what makes the church different from the world. The willingness to be filled and guided by the Spirit comes from God himself to the church (Jn 14:15-17). This disposition of the church to let the Spirit act in her midst is related to the love of the church for Christ, expressed in the keeping of his commandments. In considering this teaching of Jesus, Harry Boer has called our attention to the "retiring and self-effacing character" of the Spirit: "So it is that the loving, life-giving witnessing Spirit does not press himself on the attention of the church. He is a reticent Spirit. He remains in the background. He is content to see His love exercised, His life expressed, His witness borne forward without obtruding Himself prominently as the author of these activities."[14]

The book of Acts can be read as a development from the Gospel of John of Jesus' teaching to the apostles about the Holy Spirit. The sermons in Acts show a development in the understanding of the meaning of the person and the work of Jesus, guided and inspired by the Spirit. We see how the believers progress in their testimony to Christ in such a way that eventually in a place like Antioch they come to be called "Christians." We see also how in the midst of martyrdom, as they face death like Stephen, they are given a glimpse of the glory of Christ. We see in stories like that of Cornelius and Lydia that the Spirit has been moving, preparing people for the proclamation of the gospel, which they embrace when it comes to them.

This teaching of Jesus about the Holy Spirit in John's Gospel gives us a christological key to discern his presence and work. If the truth about Jesus Christ comes to be understood by people, so that they come to the Father through him, and if the character of Jesus Christ is reflected in their life, there we can discern the presence of the Spirit. This is the core of Christian identity; here we discover a good foundation, a cornerstone for a church that has become global and contextual in an astonishing variety of forms. Are we truly open to acknowledging as brothers and sisters in Christ people completely different from us in their theological traditions? Are we ready to take this christological core as the basis by which to discern where God's Spirit is moving today?

5. *The growth of the church in numbers and depth is the work of the Holy Spirit.* If we pay attention to the literary style of Acts we find that at crucial points in the advance of the gospel the Spirit is mentioned, so his initiative is clearly what takes the church forward. In Acts Jesus instructs the disciples to wait in Jerusalem. After Pentecost the waiting period is over, and the dynamism of the Spirit pushes the church forward. The narrative reads more like a response to an inner compulsion than to external manipulation from the leaders. The Spirit takes Philip to the road where he evangelizes and baptizes the Ethiopian eunuch (Acts 8:26-38); the Spirit opens Peter's eyes and gives him a missionary lesson he finds hard to learn (Acts 10); the Spirit moves the church in Antioch to send its best leaders on their first missionary journey (Acts 13:1-6); and when

the gospel is about to be taken into Europe, the Spirit leads Paul and Silas to Macedonia, away from the route they have planned (Acts 16:6-10). Roland Allen offers a suggestive commentary on the book of Acts: "Before Pentecost the apostles are represented as acting under the influence of an intellectual theory; after Pentecost they are represented as acting under the impulse of the Spirit."[15]

We have seen that the Spirit drives the church's advance through geographical and cultural barriers so that there is expansion and numerical growth: "The Lord added to their number daily those who were being saved" (Acts 2:47; cf. Acts 5:14; 6:7; 9:31). But the Spirit is also active in the whole life of the church, even when he is not explicitly mentioned. He fosters spiritual growth, growth in understanding the faith, growth in love and mutual acceptance, and growth in compassion for those in need. We go especially to Paul for the most explicit teaching about the activity of the Spirit in the life of the believer and the church. By the Spirit we come to faith in God and call him Father, and the same Spirit bears witness to our spirit that we are children of God (Rom 8:14-17). It is the Spirit who dwells in us and helps us to live the new life of loyalty to Christ as Lord (Rom 8:9-11); it is the Spirit who produces in us a transformation into the image of the Lord whose glory we see (2 Cor 3:17-18); it is the Spirit who produces fruit in our life, enabling us to grow in the virtues embodied in the life of Jesus: love, joy, peace, patience, kindness, generosity, faithfulness, gentleness and self-control (Gal 5:22).

In recent missiological debates around issues raised by the astonishing growth of Pentecostal and independent churches, especially among the poor, it has become necessary to have criteria for discernment. The exercise of gifts given by the Spirit makes the church grow, but the glory must go not to the gifted missionaries and evangelists but to the Lord of glory who is the giver of the gifts and the giver of growth to his church. The test to know whether a movement comes from the Spirit of God is whether such a movement glorifies Christ and continually helps to transform people into his image, making men and women more Christ-like. Evangelicals have been correct to insist that we cannot be content with the gifts of the Spirit if we do not also have the fruit of the Spirit.

LOOKING AHEAD

Evangelical theology has made an effort to keep both a missiological thrust and faithfulness to revealed truth. Our emphasis has not been on a continuity expressed by an earthly hierarchical institution but on a continuity made possible by God's Word revealed to human beings. In all the crossing of missionary frontiers, and in all the efforts at contextualization, evangelical missiology has stressed a continuity of faithfulness to the Word. In our contemporary situation we also need to pay heed to what Emil Brunner wrote halfway through the twentieth century: "It is not merely a question of the continuity of the word—the maintenance of the original doctrine—but also of the continuity of a life; that is life flowing from the Holy Ghost. The fellowship of Jesus lives under the inspiration of the Holy Spirit; that is the secret of its life, of its communion and of its power."[16] While theologians seem to be at home in handling words from the Word and in formulating precise orthodox propositions about the content of the faith, they do not know exactly how to handle the reality of the Holy Spirit at work in the church and in the world. As Brunner goes on to say, "Word and Spirit are certainly very closely connected and yet in these pneumatic energies there is something which eludes expression in words, something in relation to which all words are inadequate, if not in fact quite misleading."[17] The times call for a new openness to the Spirit.

Evangelical missions during the nineteenth and twentieth centuries, as it has been said, were more inspired by the evangelical revivals and the Moravian pioneers of mission than by the sixteenth-century magisterial reformers. The dynamism of missionary Protestantism came from the renewal movements of the eighteenth and nineteenth centuries. As Christians in these movements engaged in mission within their own context, they grasped truth about the Holy Spirit. The practical demands of their situation and their sensitivity to the Spirit allowed them to develop structures and patterns of ministry that were instrumental in accomplishing their mission. John Wesley and Count von Zinzendorf, as well as William Carey, Billy Graham and Mother Teresa, were ready to revise the old way of carrying on mission and to develop new structures adequate for the new times, because they were open to the movement of the Spirit. Recently we have become aware that beyond the people who have reached the headlines in mission history were thousands and thousands of anonymous missionaries who had that openness to go where the Spirit led them.

Brazilian missiologist Valdir Steuernagel calls for such an attitude: "Mission understood in pneumatological language is one act with two steps. It is first to perceive the blowing of the Spirit and the direction from which it comes. And then it is to run in the same direction to which the Spirit is blowing."[18] Some evangelicals (I include myself among them) think that discernment of the blowing of the Spirit requires an open attitude and sensitivity to acknowledge that his vigor may be at work even behind those things that appear new and unusual in this new stage of Christian mission. As we have seen, God's Word has much to teach on the work of the Holy Spirit sent by the Father to glorify Christ. This teaching gives us the discernment needed to feel the wind of the Spirit, and the courage and strength to unfurl our sails and let that wind take us to new shores.

8

Text and Context: The Word Through New Eyes

IT IS DINNERTIME DURING THE World Assembly of the United Bible Societies (UBS) at Mississauga, Canada, in 1996. As I sit at the table, the conversation is animated, and in spite of the variety of strange accents with which the English language is spoken, we actually communicate. I pause to reflect on people around this table: directors or board members of Bible Societies in Iceland, Peru, Mongolia, Lebanon and Spain. As we exchange stories, our imaginations move from the Amazonian jungle to the central Asian steppes, from dialogues with fundamentalist Muslims to Spanish gypsies engaged in Christian mission. The UBS is a family of 138 national organizations dedicated to the translation, production and distribution of the Bible. A typical evangelical organization in its origins, the UBS is today one of the most international and ecumenical bodies I have known. Historian A. M. Chirgwin reminds us that the modern missionary enterprise grew up side by side with this type of organization. Referring to the thirty years between 1792 and 1822, within which we find the origins of the UBS, he says that "never was there a period in which so many missionary societies and so many Bible societies came into being."[1]

Bible societies came into being because their founders wanted to share the Word of God and the gospel of Jesus Christ with all human beings. They were convinced by their own experience that God, who speaks through the Bible, gives spiritual life, and changes people, giving meaning and direction to their lives, thus forms the church as God's people, the people of the Book. We find this even in the Old Testament. When Israel went into exile and was in danger of disintegrating and disappearing as a people, the synagogue institution arose and provided the people with a sense of identity and faithfulness to God, as a testimony to other peoples and other nations. At the heart of the synagogue was the Word of God, that Older Testament that was the Bible of Jesus and Paul. When new generations of Jews experienced cultural change and lost the command of their own national language through immersion in the Greek language of the dominant culture, the Old Testament was translated into Greek, resulting in the Septuagint. Furthermore, it has been observed that while Jews, Christians and Muslims are all "people of the book," only Christians have given themselves to extensive translation of their book.

THE BIBLE IN MISSION

The Protestant Reformation in the sixteenth century was a time of intense activity in translating and spreading the Bible, and the practice of the Reformers flowed from their conviction about how God gives life, renewal and growth to the church through the Bible. The invention of printing with movable type in 1450 had made books available to the common people, and thus a new cultural artifact became the vehicle of a spiritual revolution. Chirgwin says that "nearly all the leading Reformers, however many other tasks crowded upon them, took a hand in Bible translation, and some of them made it their first priority."[2] When the Protestant missionary movement flourished two-and-a-half centuries after Luther, these principles were the source of a missionary methodology in which the translation of Scripture was a fundamental component. Historians of missions acknowledge that this practice contrasts with

Catholic missionary methodology. Stephen Neill summarizes the situation thus: "The first principle of Protestant missions has been that Christians should have the Bible in their hands in their own language at the earliest possible date. The Roman Catholic method has been different. It is not true to say that nothing had been done; we have heard of some translations of Scripture. But for the most part such literature as had been produced was made up of catechisms and books of devotion."[3]

Neill provides two examples to illustrate his point. Though Roman Catholic missionaries arrived on the Fisher Coast in South India in 1534, the first translation of the New Testament into Tamil was completed two centuries later by the Protestant Bartholomew Ziegenbalg in 1714. The first Roman Catholic missionaries arrived in the Philippines in 1565, and in three centuries a sizeable percentage of the population had been baptized. However, the first translation of a part of the Scriptures into a Filipino language—the Gospel of Luke in Pangasinan—was completed by Protestant missionaries in 1873. In 1979 I was in the Philippines taking part in Lausanne II, a congress on evangelism held in Manila celebrating fifteen years of the Lausanne movement. On television one evening a bishop in the Roman Catholic Church criticized the congress, urging Catholics not to attend the public acts related to the congress because the Roman Catholic Church was the only authorized interpreter of God's Word. As he spoke he held the Bible in front of the cameras—a copy of the translation Protestants had completed and published!

Methodist theologian José Míguez Bonino from Argentina reminds us that in Latin America during the nineteenth century and the first decades of the twentieth, the Bible played a decisive role in the rise of vigorous evangelical churches. It was not simply a book of doctrine or a devotional guide but was "the basic tool for evangelism, the seed of the church. Again and again a missionary traveled from place to place leaving Bibles, New Testaments and single books, and evangelical congregations sprang up in his trail and gathered around the Word of God. Lay preachers many times without theological or even secular education became powerful evangelists resting their authority solely on the Bible."⁴

The practice of missionaries in these cases expresses the Protestant conviction of the decisive importance of Scripture as the source of the Christian faith, the means God uses to extend his church. But in a way it also proves the deeper dimension of this conviction: the apostolic preaching as we find it in the Bible gave birth to the church and not vice versa. Because of that, the church must submit to the authority of the Word and not fall into the trap of becoming the master of the Word.

The concern to put the Bible into people's hands, in their own language, was related to the conviction that God speaks through his Word and by his Spirit in a way that the average Christian can understand. Furthermore, in understanding how to interpret Scripture, we should always keep in mind Luther's conviction of its *perspicuity*: the Bible is a clear book.

> Catholicism had maintained that the Scriptures were so obscure that only the teaching ministry of the Church could uncover their true meaning. To Luther the *perspicuity* of the Bible was coupled with the *priesthood of believers*, so that the Bible became the property of all Christians. The competent Christian was *sufficient* to interpret the Bible, and the Bible is *sufficiently* clear in content to yield its meaning to the believer. Further, the Bible was a world of its own and so *Scripture interprets Scripture.*⁵

Catholic critics viewed the Reformation principle as the opening of Christendom to every kind of anarchical tendency and revolutionary force. They saw Protestantism as the beginning of a dissolution of medieval Christianity, which they considered the only true form of Christianity. One has merely to read the works of twentieth-century historians such as Hilaire Belloc and his conservative followers, especially in the Latin countries, to see the persistence of this mindset regarding the Reformation. If such was the fear about common men and women in Europe reading the Bible, how much more when the Bible became the property of people considered "primitive" or "savage" by the average European? In fact the Bible was instrumental in reforming the sixteenth-century church in two dimensions: (1) *evangelizing* people who were only nominal Christians, and (2) *renewing* genuine Christians spiritually and morally, thus enabling them to face the challenge of the modern era opening at that historical moment.

A century after the Reformation it became evident that Protestantism itself was not immune to some of the signs of decay that the reformers had attacked in Roman Catholicism. Yet the Bible continued to be God's fundamental instrument for renewal. As Chirgwin reminds us, "The Pietist movement of the late seventeenth and early nineteenth centuries was in many respects the equivalent on the Continent of the Puritan movement in Britain and North America. Like Puritanism it had no organization; it was a movement of the Spirit and was marked by a deep devotion to the Bible and a firm belief in its evangelistic power."[6]

This was not just an academic renewal of interest in Scripture; it was also, within large Protestant bodies, the multiplication of small groups centered around a life of piety, study of Scripture and prayer. As I have already pointed out, Pietism was decisive in the development of the Moravian movement, which in turn was the source of the first concerted missionary efforts from Protestantism in the eighteenth century. Although Pietism is usually understood as an individualistic movement without social dynamism, the fact that Moravian Pietists pioneered the vast Protestant missionary work of the nineteenth and twentieth centuries should make us revise that questionable assumption. During that time Protestant missions achieved one of the most extensive advances in missionary history, and the Bible played a pivotal role in it.

In all these cases I am referring to renewal movements and missionary efforts with elements like those of the Reformation: deep spiritual experiences of individuals in their relation to God. Here spirituality becomes not only the renewal of religious life but also the source of new theological perceptions; not only the intensification of religiosity but also a new dynamism with ethical consequences at the individual and the social level. The return to Scripture, or its unlocking for the first time, illuminated the experience and thought of these peoples and movements, as can be detected in their theological tracts or treatises, in their songs and hymns, in their art and preaching.

It is also important to keep in mind other positive effects of the Protestant emphasis on Scripture. John Mackay states it perceptively: "The centrality given to the Bible in Protestant faith and experience exerted a profound influence upon those forms of cultural development which are Protestant in their inspiration. Popular interest in the Bible gave a great impulse to public education. Literacy was promoted in order that men might learn to read the Scriptures."[7] The record must be set straight at this point because many social scientists, for reasons Lamin Sanneh describes in his book, have attacked Christian missionary work: "Modern historiography has established a tradition that mission was the surrogate of Western colonialism and that together these two movements combined to destroy indigenous cultures."[8] The thrust of Sanneh's book is to show, however, that in the case of Africa, missionary work, especially the translation of the Bible into the vernacular languages, contributed to create a new sense of identity and even *resistance* to unqualified Westernization.

BIBLE AND CULTURE:
THE WORD THROUGH NEW EYES

With the existence of new, young, thriving churches that possessed the Bible in their own language, the scene was set for the rise of vigorous, fresh theological debate, for a dialogue between old and new Christian churches. The young churches needed to be able to respond to the pastoral questions that arose in their context for the penetration of their cultures with the gospel. However, it seems that just the possibility of posing the kinds of questions that Western theology had never raised became the subject of controversy. With Protestant missionary work now more than two centuries old, why is it that we have only recently witnessed the development of theologies that amount to "reading the Bible with new eyes"? Why, for so many years, was theology written by German scholars and explained by British or French professors? In his discussion of this question, Ghanaian theologian Kwame Bediako states that African students obtained advanced degrees and learned about Bultmann, Barth or Moltmann but were unable to understand the religious world in which they would conduct their ministry.[9]

At this point let us remember that the missionary movement of the nineteenth century and a good part of the twentieth was carried on within the historical framework of European and North American imperial expansion. Consciously or unconsciously, missionary action was intermingled with cultural imposition from the West. Though the Bible was given to thousands of new communities, tribes and nations in the mission fields, the way of reading the Bible communicated by the missionaries was heavily conditioned by their own culture. This retarded the possibility of gaining new insights from people of totally different cultures reading the Bible with their own eyes. Even worse, it retarded the possibility of the new churches developing a proclamation of the gospel and pastoral practices geared to their own culture and community.

As early as 1912, missiologist Roland Allen questioned the missionary methods shaped by Western ethnocentric traditions and proposed a radical change through the rediscovery and application of the apostle Paul's missionary methods.[10] A matter of special concern for Allen, in the contrast between modern mission and biblical mission, was the theological sterility and revolt that were the result of the imposition of theological patterns. He writes, "One of the most serious difficulties in the way of any spontaneous expansion and the establishment of Apostolic Churches arises from our fear for our doctrine."[11] With abundant examples he goes on to demonstrate that the European doctrinal patterns were imposed through authoritarian methods and through the financial manipulation of the new churches. He concludes that "the maintenance of our standard of doctrine by external compulsion seems to proceed through sterility to revolt."[12]

It took a series of dramatic, decisive events in the second half of the twentieth century—such as decolonization, Marxist revolutions, the emergence of new nations and reassertion of native cultures—to create among missionary practitioners and theoreticians an awareness of the need to correct imperial methods. Slowly, from the new churches in the so-called Third World, we have seen the articulation of a new way of looking at God's Word. Scottish missiologist Andrew Walls is one of the most attentive and creative observers of the development of Christianity in the non-Western world. He has tried to understand the contemporary situation in the light of the history of missions and to detect the significance of the emerging non-Western ways of looking at Scripture.

Walls has traced back through comparative historical research the manner in which the transmission of the Christian faith across cultural frontiers resulted in a series of transformations in the nature of the church and its theology. We thus see through the centuries different models of Christian life that were shaped by dynamic interaction between the Christian faith and the cultural environment in which it was planted. In the global situation of our time we should expect and accept such changes. Walls summarizes his perceptions in the question, "How does the expression of the faith compare among Temple-worshipping Jew, Greek Council Father, Celtic monk, German Reformer, English Puritan, Victorian Churchman? How defective would each think the other on matters vital to religion?"[13]

Another missiologist with experience in Africa is David Barrett. Years ago he studied in depth the phenomenal development on the African continent of hundreds of independent churches, which he sees as the explosion of a new, truly African Christianity. Barrett has pointed out the unique role played by the existence of the Bible in the language of the peoples:

It is impossible to overestimate the importance of the Bible in African society. The portions of it that are first translated are in most cases the first printed literature in the vernacular language. Vast literacy campaigns are based on it. Ability to read a Gospel is a requirement for baptism in many Protestant churches. . . . As an independent standard of reference, the scriptures have therefore provided African Christians with indispensable guidance at a crucial period at which they would otherwise have been inarticulate. So began the demand of African society for spiritual independence from the religious imperialism of Western extrabiblical ideas.[14]

When colonial control was no longer possible, this explosion resulted, which some may see as anarchy but others see as a manifestation of that power of the Word and Spirit to which the Reformation reformers referred with great hope and enthusiasm. Time, growth and advance of these young churches in their pilgrimage is bringing into fruition their theology, their way of asking questions about the faith, their agenda for global dialogue.

Here lies the relevance of the themes, questions and methods propounded by different theologies of liberation. Some of them coincide with themes and questions coming from evangelical churches around the world. If it is true that we have inherited from the Reformation our belief in the power and authority of God's Word, we cannot but rejoice in the fact that it is now translated into so many languages and revered by people from so many cultures. Those who have started to read that Word with their own eyes and respond to it must be given a hearing in the global theological dialogue. The time of European and Western monologue is over. The Lausanne Congress on Evangelism in 1974 was significant as a moment of global theological dialogue. During that event we saw how a significant segment of the evangelical community that had been deeply involved in missionary action came to understand the new situation. John Stott has expressed that new attitude eloquently:

As with the authors of Scripture, so with its readers, the Holy Spirit does not bypass our personality and teach us in a vacuum. He used the cultural background of the biblical writers in order to convey through it a message appropriate to them as real people in real situations. In the same way he uses the cultural inheritance of Bible readers to convey to them out of the Scriptures living and appropriate truth. . . . To allow and even encourage other Christians to perceive the truth of the gospel "freshly through their own eyes" is a mark both of respect for human beings and of confidence in the Holy Spirit.[15]

Writing from the context of his experience as an American missionary in the Philippines, William Dyrness has expressed well the direction and consequences for the global theological dialogue necessary today: "The day is surely past when we simply allow third world believers to 'have their say' while we Western theologians prepare the definite answers to their questions. For now we recognize that if we listen carefully we find our own assumptions challenged and our thinking sharpened." The acute question of the social conditioning of theological perception is one of the key points at which presuppositions are challenged and theological understanding may be sharpened.

In the case of evangelicals from the Third World, reading the Bible with new eyes implies first the presupposition of the revelatory nature of Scripture and its authority. Let us remember that these churches retain a fresh memory of their origin in missionary work that concentrated on the translation and announcement of the Word of God. But another important conviction has developed; namely, that they are to take seriously the unique characteristics of the cultural and historical context in which they have to minister within the realities of Asia, Africa and Latin America. This also implies the clarification of the historical conditions within which Western theological categories developed, in order to show their limitations as ways of reading Scripture. The driving thrust in this direction does not come simply from some kind of adolescent rebelliousness of younger churches or vindictive nationalism. It stems from pastoral and missionary concern. Three Asian evangelicals have expressed it in this way: "There is a growing uneasiness about the place of ready-made Western theology in an Asian context. The main concern thus is to formulate theology that is born out of the meeting of a living church and its world."[16]

They have also outlined clearly what this means in relation to the hermeneutical work of understanding Scripture, as a foundational activity for theological articulation:

> We cannot escape, epistemologically, our cultures, backgrounds and concerns, which define our mode of expression. But more than this, our theology, while thoroughly grounded in the Bible must address the concrete problems of Asia today. A penetrating study of Asia's problem is hence imperative. An Asian theology must therefore be governed by the dialectic interplay between culture and the Bible. The cultural context poses the questions to the Bible. And the biblical answer, to complete the hermeneutical circle, must be given full integrity not only to respond to the contemporary issues but especially to reformulate, if necessary the questions themselves. And these answers must then be applied to the bleeding sores of a suffering continent, or some such thing; we need to complete the *Pastoral* circle too![17]

A valuable example of how this happens is given in two steps: first, by establishing the way in which "the Western mind tends to see in reality a basic dual nature (e.g. form-matter, being-becoming, subject-object)," and then studying how that has shaped and limited theologies articulated within Greek modes of thought; second, by establishing the Eastern monistic and intuitive approach to reality to show its possibilities for a new reading of Scripture. Acknowledging that "monistic thinking is seldom applied in theology because of the predominance of dualism and the verdict that monism is in basic conflict with the Christian teaching," they propose a qualified use of a monistic frame of reference for an Asian approach to the Bible: "When monism is tempered by a healthy appreciation of the Bible dualism between Creator and creature, it can be a tool for clarity. Biblical theology suggests how a recognition of a unitary outlook in the Biblical writer's understanding of the Kingdom of God, man's psychology, etc., can qualify our own understanding of such relationships as man-creation, sacred–secular, and spirit-matter."[18]

From an angle that stresses the pastoral dimension rather than an academic one, Bishop David Gitari from the Kenyan diocese of Mount Kenya East gives us another example of this Third World evangelical approach. He first describes the conditions of his diocese, which are a good illustration of the pace of growth that characterizes the life of many African churches:

> In my own diocese, a new congregation begins at least once every month; we confirm an average of 500 candidates every Sunday. Statistics are, of course, not the best criteria for measuring church growth; growth in numbers can be deceptive. The church is faced with the problem of nurturing the Christians so that they grow in Christ and fully understand the implications of the gospel. If the gospel of Jesus Christ is to have a deep impact on the African people, so that "they may have life and have it abundantly," then we must allow the gospel to speak in the cultural situation of the Africans.[19]

He next describes the social and economic conditions of these multitudes among whom the church is growing, and how evangelists and missionaries in his diocese face the demands of the situation: "In some areas of Kenya we have recently been hit by famine. And I have personally been involved in famine relief activities." He says, "I have no doubt that the Good News of the Kingdom includes feeding the hungry." But he also makes it clear that besides relief two other things are necessary. The first is to avoid fostering an attitude of dependence on the aid giver, working with the poor instead to help them become self-sufficient: "We must go to the very roots of the cause of hunger and poverty." The second is to complete the task: "The Good News to the hungry world must not stop at giving the bread which perishes. Evangelism is the proclamation of the Good News of Jesus Christ so that people understand the message, receive him as the bread of life and are incorporated into the eucharistic life of the church."[20]

On the basis of this pastoral and evangelistic situation Gitari arrives at a new way of understanding the Bible, one closer to the reality of his own African context and to the world in which the New Testament was written. Furthermore, his situation stimulates critical perspectives on other ways of reading the text:

> In African culture, the way in which man can be man is within the family. The African culture knows no isolated individuals. Man is man because he belongs. He is a part of a larger family, a clan or a tribe. Hence John Mbiti says "I am because we are." As a member of a family man cannot be left to his own. . . . In some parts of Africa, the Christian gospel has been preached as if it were relevant only to an isolated individual. A person has to make an individual decision to accept Christ. This is an importation of individualistic cultural thinking of the West. The Philippian jailer (Acts 16) was baptized in the middle of the night with his household. Whenever an African person wants to make an important decision, he has to consult the whole family. Our evangelism in Africa must be aimed at families and groups of people.[21]

I know two missionaries who have worked creatively within this new situation. Ada Lum, from a Chinese family in Hawaii, has traveled around the world training laypeople in inductive Bible study. Working under the International Fellowship of Evangelical Students she has been able to enthuse young men and women from all continents to find for themselves in Scripture God's truth for life. Renewal has come in many churches and denominations as local congregations have come alive to Bible study through the ministry of people Ada has trained. It has been a privilege for me to accompany her in Latin America and Europe and to see her gifts in action. In Costa Rica, shortly before I wrote this chapter, I also saw Ruth Mooney, an American Baptist missionary who worked in several Central American countries and now works with women from the Atlantic coast of Costa Rica. Using inductive Bible study and the educational approach of Paolo Freire, Ruth has been able to get housewives, teachers and students to write contextual Bible study material for their churches. Besides infectious energy and dedication, Ada and Ruth have a love and enthusiasm for the Bible, an ability to put Bible scholarship to work at pew level, and great respect and sensitivity for the unique realities of the local context and for what God can do with his Word through simple people.

The life of young evangelical churches around the world is often marked by the fresh rediscovery of biblical truth characteristic of the Reformation. Under the guidance of the Holy Spirit, who has brought their communities to life through the instrumentality of the Word of God, Third World Christians are now reading Scripture with new eyes. Thus we stand at a new historical moment determined by the rise of new churches in the Third World, and this is resulting in fresh readings of Scripture as unfamiliar pastoral and missionary situations are confronted by these living communities. Finally, the new freedom in the Spirit, which enables these churches to question theological patterns developed in other cultures, also stimulates an effort to take seriously the missionary challenge posed by their own culture.

Like the two disciples who walked with Jesus on the road to Emmaus, we are a company of Christians from all over the world who now realize that Jesus Christ is at the center of all Scripture. Through missionary action and by the power of his Spirit we have received his Word, and the risen Lord has opened our eyes to the truth. Our hearts burn with joy and wonder and we have new strength to run our races, on dusty roads and paved highways, shouting the gospel at the crossroads of remote villages or sending messages through the Internet, singing it in the minor tones of Tibetan or Bolivian tunes or in the polyphonic richness of a Bach cantata.

9

Mission as Transforming Service

HIGH IN THE MOUNTAINS OF ECUADOR, at Colta, a process of rapid social change has been taking place among the Quechuas, proud descendants of the Incas. After centuries of popular religion that seemed designed to keep them submissive under an alliance of land-owners and clergy, conversion to the evangelical faith has brought a new sense of dignity, pride in their own language and a hunger for education. They have become economic agents able to accumulate savings in order to create capital and develop a network of small businesses, through which they establish reciprocal relations that enable them to face the weight of *mestizo* capitalism, still predominant in the area. These are the conclusions of anthropologist Blanca Muratorio after several years of research there.[1]

Muratorio is not a Christian and has applied Marxist tools of analysis in some aspects of her research. However, her final account traces this positive social transformation back to the way in which evangelical missionaries immersed themselves among the Quechuas, learned their language, translated Scripture into it and stayed among them with a long-term commitment to service and to accompanying them in their social pilgrimage. From the perspective of Christian mission we have here an illustration of the gospel of Jesus Christ communicating in the way Jesus did and, by the power of the Holy Spirit, transforming the lives of people and societies.

CHRISTIAN MISSION:
HUMAN AND SOCIAL TRANSFORMATION

The brief story from Ecuador is not completely new. The transforming effect of the gospel is evident in the Gospels' record of Jesus' own ministry as well as in the first history of Christian missionary work, the New Testament book of Acts. In the description of the way Jesus accomplished his mission we find a discernible pattern. For example, in the Gospel of Matthew the writer uses several brief summaries that punctuate sections of his story. Thus Matthew 9 introduces the crucial moment in which the Lord chooses his envoys, his missionaries: "Jesus went through all the towns and villages, teaching in their synagogues, preaching the good news of the kingdom and healing every disease and sickness" (Mt 9:35). This passage describes Jesus immersed among the people, ministering to their needs, and it points us clearly to the deep compassion that moved him to action (Mt 9:36-38). The crowds are not seen as numbers or faceless entities but as "sheep without a shepherd," as people who are lost because their human leaders are failing them and exploiting them. Matthew's language is taken from the forceful passage of Ezekiel 34. From this deep feeling about the needs of real people also comes the sense of missionary urgency, which is followed by the call of all disciples to pray and the call of the Twelve to their mission.

Through teaching, preaching and healing, the work of Jesus reached and transformed people in all aspects of their lives, so we can conclude without any doubt that *Jesus' mission was holistic*. His touch and teaching led to the restoration of full humanity for those to whom he ministered. His practice illustrates well the powerful statement "I have come that they may have life, and have it to the full" (Jn 10:10). Mark's Gospel narrates Jesus' healing of a demon-possessed Gerasene in a way that seems to stress the Master's transforming touch (Mk 5:1-20). This Gerasene lived in the tombs, was chained hand and foot, cried out and cut himself with stones, and could not be subdued. The description stresses the descent of a person almost to the level of the subhuman. Anyone who has been involved in mission recognizes the shocking contemporary parallels of alienated people at that level of misery and distress: for instance, drug addicts in European and North American cities, and victims of exploitation in the Third World. After the man is healed by Jesus he appears sitting, dressed and in his right mind. The man has recovered his humanity and dignity. The transformation is so radical that it brings fear to the onlookers. However, this restoration of humanity is costly, as it leads to a herd of pigs drowning. Consequently the people in that region ask Jesus to leave—a herd of pigs is more valuable than a restored human life. Redemptive missionary action through the centuries has not always been welcomed by those whose interests are at stake.

So it was with the mission of the apostles. The gospel's dramatic influence was seen not only in how it transformed individual lives but how it affected social structures. Consider the record of how the gospel penetrated the city of Philippi (Acts 16:12-40). The missionary action of Paul and Silas first reaches Lydia, a rich business executive who, as a result of conversion, consecrates her household to the missionary cause. Lydia's life cannot be understood apart from the social structure of which she is a part: her *household*, that is, her family, business, slaves. When she is touched by the gospel, social transformation occurs as all her relationships and resources are now placed at the service of Christian mission. Luke narrates, "When she and the members of her household were baptized, she invited us to her home. 'If you consider me a believer in the Lord,' she said, 'come and stay at my house.' And she persuaded us" (Acts 16:15). Later we find that Lydia's house became the meeting place for the church (v. 40).

The second person touched by the missionaries in Philippi is a poor slave girl possessed by a pythonic spirit "by which she predicted the future." She is the victim of exploitation, bringing in "a great deal of money for her owners by fortune-telling" (Acts 16:16). Slavery was an integral part of the social structure within which this girl lived. When she is spiritually liberated this structure is affected, and the reaction of her exploiters brings about social disturbance. The story shows that the slave girl's owners, whose economic advantages are challenged as a result of evangelism, develop a nationalistic, ideological accusation against the missionaries, which then results in a riot. As has happened so often in missionary history, the preaching of the gospel results in the missionaries going to jail (Acts 16:23-24).

The third person affected by the testimony of the now-imprisoned missionaries is their jailer, a hardened bureaucrat within the structure of the Roman penal system. His career could have come to a tragic end because of an earthquake, but the event opens the door of his life to the gospel and we see him transformed into a caring, serving brother in Christ (Acts 16:33-34). If we take each of these characters not only as an individual but also as a part of a structure, it is clear that the gospel challenges and changes that structure.

The gospel has a similar impact on people and structures in Ephesus (Acts 19:8-41), because in biblical mission the gospel permeates the lives of those who receive it and commit themselves to following Jesus Christ. In contexts marked by radical social change, contemporary readers can find surprising guidance and help in the details of the story so carefully told by Luke, so that texts like this provide new light for the contemporary missionary.

EVANGELICALS REDISCOVER HOLISTIC MISSION

The rediscovery of holistic mission among evangelicals in the 1960s was occasioned by the experience of churches whose evangelistic work took place in countries or social classes going through painful processes of social transformation. Latin Americans, Africans and Asians, as well as African Americans and Latinos in the United States, insisted that evangelism and mission could not be carried on in faithfulness to biblical standards unless this holistic dimension was taken into account.[2] This rediscovery may be traced to the series of congresses on evangelism initiated by the well-known evangelist Billy Graham. These were an evangelical initiative intended to explore ways in which those concerned for evangelization could join forces within the framework of a global vision. The first congress was held in Berlin in 1966 and included biblical exposition, exploration of the global context and theological affirmation, and discussion of practical approaches and methods in evangelism. A section of the program dealt with "Obstacles to Evangelism," in the course of which many participants became aware that racism, expressed in attitudes and structures, was one of the obstacles to the proclamation of the gospel. Michael Cassidy, an evangelist from South Africa, called our attention to this, and his short paper on nationalism, with its references to the apartheid in his country, stirred up great controversy.[3]

A series of regional congresses were held as a follow-up to Berlin. The 1968 United States Congress on Evangelism took place in Minneapolis at the height of the U.S. struggle for civil rights. It became evident that it was impossible to carry on evangelism while disregarding issues of social justice and structural sin. Evangelist Leighton Ford made it clear that "as Christians we have to be concerned both for love and justice." One cannot be a substitute for the other, since both are important dimensions of the gospel. As a consequence, Ford said, "A Christian politician who seeks to pass laws that create guidelines for justice is doing God's work just as truly as a Christian pastor who seeks to win the lost for Christ."[4]

The following year in Bogotá, Colombia, the Latin American Congress on Evangelism concluded that true evangelism could not take place without adequate reference to the social and political context within which it is done. Those attending indicated clearly their unanimous approval of statements like the following: "To discuss whether we should evangelize or promote social action is worthless. They go together. They are inseparable. One without the other is evidence of a deficient Christian life. So we must not try to justify service for our neighbor by claiming that it will help us in our evangelism. God is equally interested in our service and in our evangelistic task."[5]

In the Asia South Pacific Congress of Evangelism held in Singapore in 1968, the subject of the gospel and social realities was dealt with missiologically in relation to the comparison between the Christian faith and other religions. Benjamin Fernando from Sri Lanka reminded us that

> there is no such thing as a separate individual gospel and a separate social gospel. There is only one gospel—a redeemed man in a reformed society. . . . Social problems assume greater importance in Christianity than in Buddhism or Hinduism. The theory of Karma and rebirth gives a fairly reasonable explanation for social inequalities of this life which on the one hand are consequences of the previous life and on the other hand can be compensated for in the next life. But to a Christian there is only one earthly life and so social problems have to be dealt with now or never.[6]

This rediscovery of the holistic dimension of biblical teaching is a valuable example of how a Western individualistic and dualistic reading of the biblical material has been challenged by Christians from outside the West who have come to "read the Bible with their own eyes," with questions prompted by the daily life of their churches. The Asia South Pacific congress documents show how Western evangelical scholars and Bible expositors insisted on the need to go back to a more biblical and holistic view of mission and evangelism, their voices joining those of Christians from Third World churches and ethnic minorities in North America who were advocating the same course of reformation. They could point to the New Testament record of the initial missionary thrust in the first century and to historical evidence, because century after century, the history of mission is filled with stories about the transforming power of Christ, especially on the lives of the poor. The records reveal that compassion for the poor, the marginalized and the oppressed has been a distinctive mark of Christian character, modeled by Jesus himself, while also revealing the effect of the gospel on social structures: bringing help to the victims of social injustice but also challenging and sometimes transforming the evil structural roots of social injustice.

In the contemporary situation, especially in the Third World, economic development and the fight against poverty and oppression require a change of mind and lifestyle, new strength for the will to change the world, and hope to persist in spite of opposition and failure. Writing about the changes resulting from conversion in the New Testament days, Michael Green says, "The profound change which came over these men and women when they entrusted themselves to Christ affected their intellect, their conscience, their will and their subsequent life."[7] And then, writing about the Protestant movement of the sixteenth century, Swiss economist André Biéler reminds us that "the Reformation gave the leaven of the gospel back to the people. But this leaven no longer acted upon these tormented masses as a pious consolation justifying the injustices of the great and the oppression by the mighty, but rather as an energetic stimulant which gave to believers the courage to think and to speak the truth."[8]

In many contemporary mission fields, economic development projects have a better chance of success when they operate upon what we could call the spiritual infrastructure of Christian transformation. Of course, the gospel is to be preached to all human beings first and foremost because of obedience to the call of the Lord Jesus Christ, and not as a kind of subservient vehicle at the service of development schemes. However, development projects that connect with peoples and movements among whom spiritual revival is taking place have more chance of long-term success. Also, when foreign catalysts and resources have departed, these projects have more chance of becoming indigenous projects that will last. Within the framework of authentic Christian fellowship, development agents have more safeguards against paternalism. By applying biblical principles of reciprocity, solidarity and mutuality, poor Christians will be empowered to become agents of their own liberation and not passive recipients of handouts.

The city of Lima, Peru, where I am writing these lines, is now surrounded by vast accumulations of urban poor. As in other Latin American countries, they have been hit hard by the social cost of recent government programs of economic stabilization. These programs have succeeded in stopping inflation, curbing terrorism and privatizing inefficient state enterprises, but they have also created massive unemployment and destroyed social security programs that were the only resource of poor and disenfranchised people. At the worst moments of this process, thousands of Christian women in shopfront churches have been channels of help for survival, especially for children and youth. I have heard workers from a variety of nongovernmental organizations (NGOs) express admiration and praise for the stamina, joy, hope and resilience of poor, simple Christians who have faced misery and the fight for human rights in a spirit of solidarity. And there is already evidence from the process of recovery and change that these poor Christians can become important agents of development toward a new stage. It is to be hoped that they will help to construct a new type of society.

Both biblical truth and mission history provide us with solid grounds for optimism. We turn now to briefly examine New Testament teaching on the way in which the gospel is to be demonstrated.

BIBLICAL PATTERNS OF SERVICE

I find in Acts 6:1-7 a highly suggestive description of the holistic approach to mission that involves both proclamation and service within a context that appears similar to that of several mission fields today. This passage has a symmetrical structure of its own, typical of the author of Acts. The beginning (v. 1) and the end (v. 7) refer to the numerical growth of the church; in between the passage addresses a crisis brought by that growth. Throughout the passage the word *diakoneō* or words related to it appear several times. This word represents one of the three families of words in Greek usually translated as "service" in English. It is translated in the English Bible as "distribution of food" (v. 1), "wait on tables" (v. 2) and "ministry of the word" (v. 4). The activity of the apostles that was to focus on preaching was "service of the word," and the activity of those appointed to organize the distribution of food to the poor was "service of the tables."

My brief etymological excursus demonstrates that both aspects of mission were necessary and moreover that they had a common root. To perform both aspects efficiently in the fledgling Jerusalem church, a restructuring of the community's leadership was needed and was accordingly implemented.

I find here the connection with the missiological pattern offered by Jesus to which I referred above. The study of this family of words shows the degree to which the person and work of Jesus had a decisive influence on the way the authors of the New Testament developed the Greek language of their day. In the earlier, classical Greek usage, *diakoneō* meant something different, because, as H. W. Beyer wrote, "In Greek eyes serving is not very dignified. Ruling and not serving is proper to a man. . . . The formula of the sophist: 'How can a man be happy when he has to serve someone?' expresses the basic Greek attitude."[9] The person and ministry of Jesus added a new dimension to the meaning of this family of words. As Beyer says:

> Jesus' view of service grows out of the Old Testament command of love for one's neighbor which He takes and links with the command of love for God to constitute the substance of the divinely willed ethical conduct of His followers. In so doing He purifies the concept of service from the distortions which it had suffered in Judaism. Jesus' attitude to service is completely new as compared with the Greek understanding. The decisive point is that He sees in it the thing which makes a man His disciple.[10]

The significant difference between what service meant in the Greek culture and what it came to mean in New Testament usage was possible only because a man named Jesus existed and had a strong impact on the memory of a community and the culture created by that community.

When the New Testament writers try to elucidate the reality of Jesus' life in order to grasp the meaning of that life, they find their best point of reference in the servant songs of the prophet Isaiah. As pointed out earlier in this book, one characteristic of Jesus was his self-consciousness, his clear sense of identity with the Father. Also, it was not enough for him merely to act in a particular way; he needed to explain his actions. Jesus fed the multitudes, healed the sick and befriended marginalized people, but he also preached and taught.

Let me give an example of how this might translate into the present. I have great respect for the relief and development work of the Mennonite Central Committee, a North American organization that channels the social work of twenty-two Anabaptist families of churches, including the Mennonites and Church of the Brethren. Their volunteers work in the most difficult situations, for which their advocacy of peace and their tradition of communal life, frugality and service are valuable assets. That tradition has been nourished by a Christology that has insisted on the lordship of Jesus Christ and the validity of his example for discipleship today. I respect their ecumenical concerns and their reluctance to evangelize parts of Latin America, Asia and Africa, where other churches are at work, but I also believe that providing relief and service cannot be divorced from evangelism, because the world needs both their presence and their proclamation.

The test of missionary faithfulness to Jesus will be not only the practice of certain virtues and the embodiment of certain attitudes but also the proclamation of the Name that makes them possible. The service (*leitourgia*) of naming and worshiping the Servant Messiah is essential for grasping the real dimensions of living as his followers. In Acts 6 there is a division of labor, but in the following chapters, those like Stephen who had been appointed to "serve the tables" proved to be outstanding and courageous "servants of the word." In fact, the gifts required from those selected to serve the tables were not only their natural gifts of leadership but also the fullness of the Spirit, which enabled them to engage in holistic missionary action. Leaving the naming, worshiping and proclaiming of Jesus to specialized missionaries while others specialize only in acts of service may be a way of moving the division of labor too far away from the biblical model. This world is crying out for more servant-evangelists and more evangelist-servants after the pattern of Jesus.

WORD AND DEED HAND IN HAND

The dialogue of practitioners and theologians after the Lausanne congress has provided a valuable structure for holistic mission in the future, clarifying the theological basis for it as well as the ways in which proclamation and service relate to one another. The Grand Rapids Report puts it like this: "For the gospel is the root of which both evangelism and social responsibility are the fruits. As good news of love in Christ, the gospel demands both to be preached and to be lived. Once we have come to know it we are obliged to share it with others and to 'adorn' it by good deeds (Tit 2:10)."[11] The document establishes the trinitarian basis for both mission and social concern, declaring that we believe in a God of justice who in every community hates evil and loves righteousness, and a God of mercy who, according to the psalmist, "executes justice for the oppressed" and "gives food to the hungry" (Ps 146:7 NRSV). It further emphasizes how the missionary style of Jesus "reflected this lovingkindness of God his Father" and reminds us that the first fruit of the Holy Spirit is love (Gal 5:22). "It is therefore he who gives his people a tender social conscience, and impels them to immerse themselves in humanitarian relief, development and the search for justice."[12]

Missionaries will also find helpful the threefold relationship of evangelism and social concern within holistic mission that this document established and that I illustrated with several examples earlier in this chapter.

First, social activity is a *consequence* of evangelism. In fact, social activity is one of the principal aims of evangelism, for Christ gave himself for us not only to "redeem us from all iniquity" but also to "purify for himself a people of his own who are zealous for good deeds" (Tit 2:14 NRSV).

Second, social activity can be a *bridge* to evangelism, because "it can break down prejudice and suspicion, open closed doors and gain a hearing for the gospel."[13]

Third, social activity accompanies evangelism as a *partner*, as evident in the public ministry of Jesus: "They are like the two blades of a pair of scissors or the two wings of a bird."[14]

There is one more way in which regard for the theological basis of holistic mission is a safeguard against error. In many parts of the world a flawed "prosperity theology" has become popular, especially among the poor. There are American, German, South African, Korean and Brazilian variations of this theology, which is propagated through marketing techniques. The idea is that acceptance of the gospel brings immediate personal success, health and wealth; that sickness is always the result of lack of faith; and that getting the luxuries of the consumer society is simply a matter of naming and claiming in prayer. Prosperity theology of this kind has no regard for the social responsibility of the Christian. As we have seen throughout this chapter, the gospel changes people; many times that change brings a measure of prosperity. But we must never forget that conversion to Jesus Christ may also bring persecution and suffering, and a biblically based prosperity that takes seriously the character of God, Jesus Christ and the Holy Spirit will always be accompanied by a new sense of solidarity and love for one's neighbor. It is well summed up in the advice of the apostle Paul to the Ephesians: "Thieves must give up stealing; rather let them labor and work honestly with their own hands, so as to have something to share with the needy" (Eph 4:28 NRSV). The gospel not only infuses people with new life and gives them a capacity to work honestly and save for a more ordered and comfortable life, but it also transforms the social conscience, so that believers gladly learn "to share with the needy."

Summing up, then, mission as service in Jesus' name involves proclamation of the gospel of salvation; life in fellowship in the body, which is the church; worship and prayer in Jesus' name; and the multiplicity of tasks Jesus' disciples perform in response to human needs. Mission is patterned on the example and saving death of Jesus, who, in his own words, "did not come to be served, but to serve, and to give his life as a ransom for many" (Mt 20:28). In the twenty-first century the scene around the world seems similar to the events narrated in the chapters of Acts explored here. The church is experiencing new growth pains in Africa, Asia, eastern Europe and Latin America, where vast numbers of Western volunteers from Christian NGOs spend their time and talents. The world that surrounds the growing church is not Christendom, where the values and virtues of nominal Christianity were once present. Rather, the values of postmodern as well as some premodern societies are those of a competitive and cruel jungle. The attitudes of consumerist elites in the West and of corrupt ruling autocrats in some Third World nations are closer to those of the Greeks in the time before Jesus, God's supreme Servant, came. Today mission should consist of service—service both of the spiritual in proclaiming the Word and of the physical in meeting human needs, according to Jesus' model and in his name. In this new era of globalization this means new patterns of cooperation and new forms of partnership for mission. We shall explore them in the next chapter.

A New Way of
Looking at the World

ARMED WITH HIS BIBLE AND WITH the best medical training a prestigious American university could give him, Daniel Fountain went to Zaire as an American Baptist medical missionary. After almost thirty years of medical practice in Africa, he returned a changed man. In the course of a life of service he had to unlearn some of the things the university had taught him about human nature, and his eyes were opened to new perspectives from his brothers and sisters in Africa. His book *Health, the Bible and the Church* is the result of a year of reflection on his practice, and it describes his new and refreshing understanding of what the Bible teaches about human beings. It is a forceful call to change the way in which we regard human beings. Fountain says, "Secular philosophy ignores or even denies the realm of the spirit because it is beyond the limits of scientific experimentation. Life has no ultimate meaning and God has become irrelevant to any considerations of health and healing."[1] But in his medical practice he found that much illness and "dis-ease" come precisely from that loss of meaning and purpose, so he could not avoid the conclusion that "if the sick person is to be made whole, we must involve in the restoration process the center of the personality where the quest for meaning and purpose exist."[2]

Through missionary practice and reading the Bible, Fountain discovered *a new way of looking at the world*. His experience is a good illustration
of a powerful statement from the apostle Paul about the way in which an
encounter with Jesus Christ changes our perspective: "So from now on
we regard no one from a worldly point of view" (2 Cor 5:16). This statement is followed by a reference to the source of this new perspective
when Paul writes, "even though we once knew Christ from a human
point of view, we know him no longer in that way. So if anyone is in
Christ, there is a new creation: everything old has passed away; see, everything has become new!" (2 Cor 5:16-17 NRSV). As F. F. Bruce comments, "an appreciation of Christ crucified involves a transvaluation of
values and in particular the turning upside down of secular canons of
wisdom and power."[3]

Fountain's self-critical observations concerning medical practice
could also be applied to counseling, teaching, pastoral and missionary
work. "For many reasons we have lost the art of communication. . . .
Medical specialists can repair, alter or prop up the human body with
great skill and we even have a growing supply of 'spare parts.' Yet we
seem unable to touch the human spirit or bring wholeness to the sick
person."[4] He found that doctors "depersonalize" sick people into "pa-
tients" and make them objects for study and treatment. He says that the
scientific training that teaches doctors to think objectively has made the
doctor-patient relationship a nonreciprocal one. "Because we cannot
measure relationships, they are not 'scientific.' So we do not consider the
family or social contexts either as etiological factors in the development
of disease nor as possible therapeutic allies in the healing process."[5]

Missionaries too must be on guard against practices that "depersonalize" others, turning them into "unreached" entities to be "targeted" for
evangelism. In this way "the unreached" become faceless objects we use
to fulfill our plans and prove the effectiveness of our strategies. I value
the effort to find out where the gospel is most needed through the use of
the enormous amounts of data now available about peoples and places.

But this can easily turn into a "technique" that satisfies the thirst for scientific precision in the handling of people that is characteristic of the West and some Westernized Asian societies. Biblical missionary work, like true medicine, establishes reciprocal relationships, because missionaries themselves are people, not just technicians. Consequently they are truly respectful of the freedom and dignity of those people to whom they go as missionaries. They are open to the way in which, in the midst of missionary action, God can transform both the missionaries themselves as well as those whom they want to serve and reach in mission. Mission needs a continual recovery of the biblical view of people.

Sharing with his readers a great number of experiences from his missionary practice, Fountain also takes us into an exploration of the Bible's teaching about people, health, illness, wholeness and even food. As he ponders years of experience, we come to understand better one of his conclusions:

> The biblical world view is the framework we receive from God's Word, the Bible, and from Jesus Christ. This is the framework into which we as Christians must fit our thinking, our ways of doing things and our judgments. The secular world view on the other hand, is the framework we have developed from human wisdom, reason and observation alone and which depends only on them. We need to understand the fundamental differences between these two world views.[6]

In the mission field, medical practice along the line of current canons of Western medicine proved insufficient for Fountain. Compelled by the cry of human need and his own commitment to serve people, he rediscovered the relevance of the biblical view of people. He rediscovered a holistic view of people that includes the spiritual dimension of life.

FROM MISSION TO THEOLOGY

There is a connection between Fountain's conclusions and Paul's statement in 2 Corinthians 5, "From now on we regard no one from a worldly point of view," which is written within a missionary context. Although Paul had had a wrong conception of the Messiah, or perhaps a wrong conception of Jesus of Nazareth (2 Cor 5:16), when he came to understand the reconciling love of Jesus Christ in his death and resurrection (2 Cor 5:14-15), Paul had not only a new vision of Christ but also a new way of looking at human beings. Equality before God beyond cultural and ethnic borders is the dimension of the human that Paul found in Christ. As Ajith Fernando comments, "Race, class, caste and education are all insignificant in the light of the amazing thing that God has done, the light of which is so strong that other human factors pale into insignificance."[7]

Second Corinthians deals at several points with Paul's missionary style, born out of his Christology, and it is consistent with the teaching of other Pauline writings. In Christ a new humankind emerges in the encounter of Greek and barbarian, wise and foolish, Jew and Gentile, master and slave, male and female. At the core of the sense of call that grips Christians to engage in missionary action is a fundamental change of outlook operated by an encounter with Jesus Christ, a transformation that leads us to regard "the other" in a different manner. For Christians today this means accepting those who are different from us as creatures of God, who loves them and wants to reach them with the good news of the gospel. Such was the case of the apostle Peter. He was called by God to cross ethnic and cultural borders in order to take the gospel to the Roman centurion Cornelius. In the process his vision, and thus his theology, was enlarged and transformed; he confessed that "it is unlawful for a Jew to associate with or to visit a Gentile," yet "God has shown me that I should not call anyone profane or unclean" (Acts 10:28 NRSV).

This change of perspective, this new way of looking at other people, provoked tensions in the early church. As the gospel crossed geographical and cultural frontiers, the missionary met with "the other" in a new way. Going back to 2 Corinthians, Paul's practical teaching on the life of the church proves that he did not shrink from dealing with thorny theological and pastoral issues brought by transcultural encounter. Thus, during the Pax Romana (27 B.C.-A.D. 180), the usual Greek, Jewish or Roman ways of regarding people were confronted by those of the missionary. And in the world of the twenty-first century the worldly secular way is again challenged by the rediscovery of a new way. From the frontier of missionary life comes the debate that both challenges secular norms and revitalizes theology.

Other voices coming from missionary experience are also calling us to question seriously the contemporary secular worldview. I think of the respected anthropologist Charles H. Kraft, former missionary and Bible translator in Africa, and professor at Fuller Seminary's School of World Mission in Pasadena, California. In his book *Christianity with Power*, subtitled *Your Worldview and Your Experience of the Supernatural*,[8] Kraft's starting point is his charismatic experience related to the controversial course "Signs and Wonders" that John Wimber taught at Fuller Seminary in the early 1980s. He traces his encounter with the Holy Spirit back to his frustrating experiences in Nigeria. Christian leaders there were well aware of the confrontation with spiritual powers in their religious experience, but missionaries shaped by a secularist worldview could be of no help to them. "We had brought an essentially powerless message to a very power-conscious people," says Kraft.[9]

Some of the issues raised by Kraft's experiences within the structure of the "signs and wonders" movement in California demand theological and pastoral discernment in order to be evaluated adequately. But I think that, apart from our way of perceiving his experiences, Kraft's contribution as an anthropologist is important in revising the development of our post-Enlightenment worldview and highlighting the need to come out of its captivity if a consistent Christian worldview is going to be operative in our lives and ministry. Kraft alerts us to the fact that

> the majority of the creative minds in Western societies largely ignore the spiritual nature of humans or confuse it with our psychological makeup.

And the possibility of nonhuman spiritual beings in the universe who can really make a difference is generally considered fiction. As humans we are understood to be the products of natural processes such as evolution and sexual relations. The concept of humans made in the "image of God" seems puzzling, even to many Christians.[10]

Fountain and Kraft, each in their own way and probably without being aware of their coincidences, have done the kind of theological work that the great missiologist Lesslie Newbigin outlined in his Warfield Lectures at Princeton Theological Seminary in 1984, published later under the title *Foolishness to the Greeks: The Gospel and Western Culture.* "There is no higher priority for the research of missiologists," said Newbigin, "than to ask the question of what would be involved in a genuinely missionary encounter between the gospel and this modern Western culture."[11] It is evident for Newbigin that such a priority is urgent not only for those who deal with the missionary crossing of frontiers in other lands but also for pastors, evangelists and seminary professors who have to deal with the missionary encounter in the United States or Europe. Newbigin came to the formulation of such an agenda, as mentioned earlier, after spending thirty years as a missionary in India and then returning to England to minister in a parish of factory workers. There he experienced the outcome of the secularization process that, during his absence, had made deep inroads in the culture of his country. Newbigin describes how Western missionaries in our time have come to share in the general loss of confidence in modern Western culture: "They have become more aware of the fact that in their presentation of the gospel they have often confused culturally conditioned perceptions with the substance of the gospel and thus wrongfully claimed divine authority for the relativities of one culture."[12]

What Newbigin found surprising was that in all the missiological literature about contextualization there was no serious reflection about "the fact that Western culture had become resistant to the gospel." The fact was that while the church grew in vast areas of Asia, Africa and Oceania, in areas where Western culture was predominant, Newbigin reported, "the church is shrinking and the gospel appears to fall on deaf ears."[13]

Besides setting the missiological agenda, Newbigin contributed to the task by critically evaluating the Enlightenment and its influence on Western theology. Newbigin reviews briefly several theologies, among them the kind of liberal theology

> in which the boundaries of what is possible to believe were firmly fixed by the axioms of the Enlightenment, in which it was taken for granted that the modern scientific worldview provides the only reliable account of how things really are, and that the Bible has to be understood only in terms of that account. This required a reconstruction of biblical history on the lines of modern historical science. It required the elimination of miracle.[14]

Fountain and Kraft coincide with Newbigin in their criticism of the reductionist view of people that comes from yielding to the worldview of the Enlightenment. However, they do not deny the value of science in certain fundamentalist theologies. By means of their practice and experience, they show the limitations of a secularist worldview and stress the need to make room for the human dimensions to which the message of the Bible points. The Lausanne Covenant places this issue as an aspect of the spiritual conflict involved in mission:

> We acknowledge that we ourselves are not immune to worldliness of thought and action, that is to a surrender to secularism. For example, although careful studies of church growth both numerical and spiritual are right and valuable, we have sometimes neglected them. At other times, desirous to ensure a response to the gospel, we have compromised our message, manipulated our hearers through pressure techniques, and become unduly preoccupied with statistics or even dishonest in our use of them. All this is worldly. The church must be in the world, the world must not be in the church. (par. 12)

BEYOND PROVINCIALISM

Western societies have become mission fields, and this new way of looking at the world, gained by missionaries in the course of their service, will be an important factor in the reevangelizing of the West. Newbigin, Kraft and Fountain belong to a breed of missionary that went to the mission field not only to teach but also to learn, to be enriched by fellowship and partnership with their coworkers, brothers and sisters in other cultures and places. Their writings and attitude show that instead of imposing an Anglo-Saxon package of methods and systems on India or Africa, they went to serve and to learn, and they brought back insights and perspectives that enriched the life of their home churches. Some missiologists call this "mission in reverse," while others use the image of a two-way street to describe the dynamics of the process.

As we enter a new phase in the history of Christian mission, now with a truly global church, the time has come to revise all kinds of provincialism that have characterized the relationship between churches new and old, rich and poor, North and South. There is the kind of provincialism of people like myself, who, as a Latin American Baptist, at first would not consider liturgical order, infant baptism, clerical gowns or Episcopal authority as compatible with an evangelical stance. Contact and fellowship with Lutheran and Anglican brothers and sisters who hold evangelical convictions and are involved in missionary work in different parts of the world have widened my horizons, helping me to see new dimensions of the way in which the Spirit of God has worked in history and is at work today.

Because of my experience in Latin America I never had a provincial attitude toward my Pentecostal brothers and sisters. Their zeal for evangelism and a holy life was vital in the development of evangelical student work in my part of the world. My difficulty was with Christians from the older European liturgical churches. Could the Holy Spirit really be at work in them? However, I have had to meet the opposite kind of provincialism from old, liturgical established churches that find it difficult to believe that the Holy Spirit may be at work in the noisy, exuberant forms of worship and evangelism practiced by Pentecostal or independent churches in the Southern Hemisphere, or among the poor and marginalized peoples in North America and Europe.

I also think of other kinds of provincialism. I remember a theological discussion I attended in Grand Rapids, Michigan, where a minister from the Reformed tradition told me that the pacifist stance of a Mennonite student from Ethiopia was evidence that she had not been taught good evangelical hermeneutics. I think of my own puzzlement when I attended a Messianic Assembly in Jerusalem that met on Saturdays and followed the Old Testament readings of the Jewish rabbis but whose leaders asked me not to use the word *Christian*. Talking with some of these Jewish believers, I found they could not conceive of other ways of following Jesus. The people I mention in these examples are all deeply committed to the missionary obligation of the church and active in it. Could all these mutually excluding provincialisms be practiced by people who had been saved by the same Lord, by the power of the same Holy Spirit? Those of us who confess the evangelical faith need to revise provincial attitudes if we are to gain a better understanding of the global church and a more concerted participation in global mission in the future.

I have taken the term *provincialism* from David Shank, a Mennonite missionary who spent twenty-three years as a missionary in Belgium and thirteen years in the Ivory Coast. He reminds us that "today Africa holds, without rival, the distinction of being the place where the largest number of people moved into the Christian stream of history in the shortest amount of time."[15] Since 1959, North American Mennonites have related to a large number of the independent churches in Africa that have become known by the technical name of African-Initiated Churches (AICS). The aim was not to make them Mennonite but to partner with them for mission in Africa. Shank writes, "We in the West are entering an era when we must learn to listen to what our brothers and sisters around the globe have to tell us. The nature of the world church requires it. Christ's new commandment to love one another calls for a reciprocity that goes beyond the motley band of Twelve."[16] According to Shank, Mennonites have learned much from the AICS. He lists six lessons: (1) the faith of the powerful is irrelevant, and mission has to be characterized by servanthood, (2) the gospel is a source of liberating power, (3) faith is a spiritual combat, (4) the Western interpretation of Scripture is not the final word, (5) God is experienced as an awe-inspiring divine mystery and (6) the power of the faith community is in the laity.[17]

NEW PARTNERSHIPS FOR MISSION

Global partnership of churches will be indispensable for mission in the twenty-first century. Among evangelicals this conviction grew in the last quarter of the twentieth century. During the Lausanne Congress of Evangelism in 1974, evangelicals reached a consensus that global Christian mission had become the responsibility of a global church, not only the privilege of the Western missionary enterprise. As the Lausanne Covenant states it, "We rejoice that a new missionary era has dawned. The dominant role of western missions is fast disappearing. God is raising up from the younger churches a great new resource for world evangelization, and it is thus demonstrating that the responsibility to evangelize belongs to the whole body of Christ" (par. 8). The Covenant asked all churches to participate in global mission and to reevaluate their role. These new forms of partnership were not only urgent from a practical perspective; they had theological and testimonial significance: "Thus a growing partnership of churches will develop and the universal character of Christ's church will be more clearly exhibited" (par. 8). In the face of the urgency of the task, owing to the fact that "more than two-thirds of mankind have yet to be evangelized," the Covenant urges churches and parachurches to pray and to launch new mission efforts.

The Covenant unfolds some of the consequences of taking seriously the new missionary era that has dawned: "Missionaries should flow ever more freely from and to all six continents in a spirit of humble service.

The goal should be by all available means and at the earliest possible time, that every person will have the opportunity to hear, understand and receive the good news" (par. 9). A note of realism follows in a warning and a call that are especially relevant to our subject: "We cannot hope to attain this goal without sacrifice. All of us are shocked by the poverty of millions and disturbed by the injustices which cause it. Those of us who live in affluent circumstances accept our duty to develop a simple life-style in order to contribute more generously to both relief and evangelism" (par. 9).

Almost thirty years after these words were issued the reference to shocking poverty as well as the call to a simple lifestyle have become more relevant than ever to our discussion of global partnership for mission. Globalization has facilitated communication to the point that material and technological means are now available to create and develop transnational and transcontinental partnerships for the recruitment, training and sending of missionaries. On the other hand, the growth of economic and social disparities adds difficulties to the development of effective global partnerships.

Fifteen years after Lausanne, missiologist Larry Pate gathered data about the dynamic involvement of Third World churches in global Christian mission. Pate described dramatically the agony of Western missions facing restrictions by countries that were closing their borders to missionaries, as well as the growing activity of resurgent religions. However, he counterbalanced this with a glowing report about "the burgeoning growth of missions by Christians in the Two Thirds world." He stated clearly that "a large part of the future of mission belongs to the missionaries of Latin America, Africa, Asia and Oceania."[18] He also offered statistics showing the steady growth of that missionary movement, some valuable case studies and a directory of Third World agencies that were sending missionaries to other parts of the world.

There has been a continuous and steady growth in this intentional missionary activity from the non-Western countries. The records we have are approximate and need to be qualified, but they show significant growth. Anyone who attends missionary conferences, missionary celebrations or missiological gatherings knows that the presence of representatives of young and flourishing mission organizations from the non-Western world has become increasingly evident in North America and Europe. We have growing numbers of nationals sent by non-Western agencies involved in pioneering missionary situations among Muslim, Buddhist or animistic peoples, and we also have more non-Westerners involved in the new evangelization of Europe and North America, and in the promotion and training of traditional Western mission agencies. Taking an example from Latin America, the figures compiled by Pate showed that the number of sending agencies had gone from 61 in 1972 to 92 in 1980 and 150 in 1988. The estimated number of missionaries sent from Latin America had risen from 820 in 1972 to 1,127 in 1980 and 3,026 in 1988.[19] The most recent study available shows that by 1997 there were 284 Protestant sending agencies and a total of 3,921 missionaries in Latin America.[20]

At first this growth was spontaneous; it was not a response to the mobilizing techniques that Western agencies may have developed. As I have said elsewhere in this book, missionary vision and drive have always been connected in history to movements of spiritual revival. Missionary attitudes mark young churches where the memory of their origin is still fresh, but also old churches when they are shaken and revitalized. The spiritual vitality of people, churches and denominations in times of revival has nourished the vision and the willingness to obey Christ, and so has made possible great advances in mission. Revival has been the cradle of missionary vocations and the kind of environment in which new structures for mission have been imagined. The sheer numerical weight of a church does not produce missionary vocations naturally or logically. Catholics in Latin America are concerned by the fact that though half the Catholics of the world live in Latin America, only 2 percent of the Catholic missionary force comes from that region.[21] Commenting on the words of the prophet, "O Jehovah, revive thy work in the midst of the years" (Hab 3:2 ASV), Paul Hiebert has stated it precisely: "Any long range vision for missions must include not only the planting of new churches but also the renewal of old ones. The former without the latter eventually leads only to lands full of dead and dying churches. The birth of new congregations is no guarantee that they will remain spiritually alive."[22]

The sense of urgency about evangelization in places where the gospel has not been preached yet and an effort to formulate a long-range vision for mission are distinctive notes of the missiological school I describe as "managerial missiology." Its basic tenet is that Christian mission can be reduced to a "manageable enterprise" thanks to the use of information technology, marketing techniques and managerial leadership.Their effort to visualize the missionary task with "scientific" precision has led to the formulation of concepts such as "unreached peoples," "homogeneous units," the "10-40 window" or "adopt-a-people."[23] These concepts and techniques need the correction that comes from a biblical view of people. What I am seeing in the application of these concepts in the mission field is that missionaries "depersonalize" people into "ureached targets," making them objects of hit-and-run efforts to get decisions that may be reported. Missionaries from a large American mission board that has adopted managerial missiology are now running up and down Latin American countries with their portable computers and programs to find the "unreached," with no time or energy left to relate with their denominational brothers and sisters about partnership in missionary service. The difficult tasks of discipleship and building the body of Christ are bypassed in the name of managerial goals that seem designed to give their missionary center in the United States an aura of success.

THE NEW HUMANITY IN BIBLICAL PERSPECTIVE
Global partnerships for mission, as the first fruits of the new humanity God is creating, will be a tangible expression of the biblical vision of the

church. In a fragmented, hopeless world a powerful testimony to the reality of God's reign will be offered by the continuity of Christian mission through agencies that in their makeup and policies express the universality of the gospel. The vision of the people of God as a fellowship of disciples who have been transformed by the power of the gospel and who live in a way that challenges the values of the world is a vision rooted in the New Testament practice and teaching on mission. The church is called to be an instrument of God for mission, a missionary people, a community of transformed people who live as a new fellowship, a sign of the reign of God at work in the midst of human history. As Padilla has expressed it, "The missiology that the church needs today ought to be perceiving the people of God not as a quotation that simply reflects the society of which it is a part but as 'an embodied question mark' that challenges the values of the world."[24]

Much of the New Testament material can be read as the description of the crisis provoked by the first great step in transcultural mission and the way in which the apostles coped with it. As the gospel moved from the Jewish into the Gentile world, missionary responsibility passed from the homogeneous first generation of Jewish believers to the heterogeneous communities in the Greco-Roman world. The apostle Paul was chosen by God as the champion of this great missionary step that has a paradigmatic value for the church through the ages. Luke's writings reflect Paul's convictions and practice. Other writings, like those of John, show other dimensions of the same development. In the biblical vision of reality are unique elements that cannot be pressed into the mold of contemporary worldviews but stand in creative tension with them. The church is the community that lives by the biblical vision. The church proclaims in worship as well as in service, message and lifestyle that the existence of the universe and human history can make sense and be understood only within the purpose of God manifested in Jesus Christ by the power of the Holy Spirit. Again, Padilla expresses it eloquently: "With the coming of Jesus Christ all barriers that divide humankind have been broken down and a new humanity is now taking shape *in* and *through* the church."[25] Because the church sees its own existence as the fulfillment of that biblical vision and lives by it, it is a community which embodies that creative tension, with all the contradictions and agonies this involves.

With its unprecedented technological and economic dynamism, the globalization process in our time places before us burning issues of race and culture, ethnicity and multiculturalism, justice and peace. A global church developing new partnerships for mission faces an impossible task, but God is the God of the impossible. In a commentary on the book of Revelation, Justo González reminds us that the challenges before us are similar to those faced by the New Testament church of the Roman Empire. He points especially to the challenge of multiculturalism that exists not only in society but also within the church, and says:

> How we deal with that challenge is crucial to the church and its mission. . . . First and foremost if the Christian community is to be a city set on a hill, or a beacon guiding the world into God's future, its own inner life must point the way toward that future. If the Christian gospel is not powerful enough within the church itself to lead us through the difficulties of ethnic conflict and cultural dissonance we can hardly claim that it is good news to a world going through similar difficulties on a much larger scale. The church must be one, not primarily for its own sake—or its own order, its own sense of security, etc. The church must be one because a fragmented church is not much help to a fragmented world.[26]

One of the dominant themes of the book of Revelation is worship, understood in the rich biblical sense that includes doing justice and rejecting idolatry. Part of the new way of looking at the world found in Revelation is the hopeful look at humankind that John of Patmos expresses, where "a great multitude that no one could count, from every nation, from all tribes and peoples and languages" (Rev 7:9 NRSV) stands in adoration before the Lamb. This suggests that as we engage in acts of missionary obedience to the Lamb and as we worship him in our local churches and serve him in global partnerships, we move in the direction to which God is pointing us:

> Worship is also an act of rehearsal. It is an anticipation of things to come. It is the moment at which we are reminded that our lives and our world have a goal, and that this goal is that day when every nation and tribe and people and language will worship God and the Lamb. It must be a foretaste, within our small community of worship of that great city, the New Jerusalem, which John saw coming down from heaven, from God. It is practice for the Kingdom. It is a foretaste of the Reign of God.[27]

For Further Study

AN INTRODUCTORY BOOK ON CHRISTIAN MISSION is like an appetizer: it is an effort to inform those interested in questions posed by the practice of mission and contemporary trends in reflection on that practice. It suggests but cannot go too far in developing an agenda. In these final pages I share information about the sources of wisdom that have helped my own missionary practice and teaching of mission courses in various places and contexts.

To begin with, practitioners of mission appreciate missiological reflection better than those with no missionary experience. Classes I have taught became lively laboratories when students who were missionaries on furlough or who had recently visited mission work confronted writers and speakers with burning questions from their practice. As I have said at several points in this book, the missiological approach to Scripture, history or the social sciences makes more sense and has a clear direction when it relates to a practice that provides an agenda for systematic study. It is understandable that missionaries may feel impatient or skeptical about academic mission studies that do not connect with life. At the same time, activists need continual reminders that a practice that is not placed periodically under the light of God's Word may become the ritual perpetuation of a tradition that is fruitless from the perspective of God's kingdom.

Mission studies have developed significantly in both quantity and quality during recent decades. Phenomenal growth has accompanied developments in mission history, so we can say that such history at its best has been a good case of reflection on praxis. Mission studies register also the widening and deepening of their agenda, which is required by the slow but irreversible process of Christian mission globalization. However, most of the publishing of missiological material is still done in English and in the West, and this chapter is evidence of that fact. Several of the books featured here have contributors from around the world but are published by North American and European publishers. I acknowledge the limitations of this effort, but for all practical purposes English is the lingua franca at the beginning of this new era of globalization.

DIALOGUES

Missiological literature shows how the relation between theory and practice has facilitated conversation and exploration of divergences and convergences among evangelicals, ecumenical Protestants, Orthodox Christians and Roman Catholics. The ongoing dialogue takes place in organizations such as the International Association of Mission Studies, the American Society of Missiology and the Overseas Ministries Study Center. Important documents, such as the report of the *Evangelical-Roman Catholic Dialogue on Mission 1977-1984*, edited by John R. W. Stott and Basil Meeking (Eerdmans and Paternoster, 1986); and the World Council of Churches statement on *Mission and Evangelism: An Ecumenical Affirmation*, compiled and edited by Jean Stromberg (World Council of Churches, 1983), have resulted from this dialogue.

In the same section may be placed compilations of missiological texts and documents from a variety of traditions that James A. Scherer and Stephen B. Bevans are publishing under the general title *New Directions in Mission and Evangelization*. Volume one (Orbis, 1992) deals with basic statements from conferences, congresses and study groups between 1974 and 1991, and volume two (Orbis, 1994) organizes fifteen essays in sections on the nature of mission, historical background, missionary praxis, the study of mission and documentation. The subject of volume three (Orbis, 1999) is faith and culture.

An excellent collection of documents from the evangelical dialogue and reflection related to the Lausanne Movement is *Making Christ Known: Historic Mission Documents from the Lausanne Movement 1974-1989*, edited and introduced by John R. W. Stott (Eerdmans and Paternoster, 1996).

REFERENCE BOOKS

A variety of sources and perspectives are usually represented in dictionaries. For those people starting to explore the vast field of mission studies, these are more valuable than space and time allow me to address here.

A course on mission could be organized around *Mission Legacies* (Orbis, 1994). Edited by Gerald H. Anderson, Robert T. Coote, Norman A. Horner and James M. Phillips, it offers seventy-five "biographical studies of leaders of the modern missionary movement." Promoters, interpreters, theologians, historians, theorists, strategists and administrators are included, as well as missionaries who worked in Africa, China and southern Asia. The editors mention the possibility of an additional volume that will include mission leaders associated with North Africa, the Middle East, Northeast Asia, the Pacific and Latin America. Gerald H. Anderson is also the editor of the *Biographical Dictionary of Christian Missions* (Eerdmans, 1999), which includes articles on twenty-four hundred outstanding people in the history of missions, representing Roman Catholic, Orthodox, Anglican, Protestant, Pentecostal and indigenous churches. The contributors represent 349 countries. An extremely valuable work in the American Society of Missiology series is *Dictionary of Mission: Theology, History, Perspectives,* edited by Karl Müller, Theo Sundermeier, Stephen Bevans and Richard Bliese (Orbis, 1997).

Though a more restricted and defined focus was intended in the *Dictionary of Pentecostal and Charismatic Movements*, edited by Stanley M. Burgess, Gary B. McGee and Patrick H. Alexander (Zondervan, 1988), one finds in it people and movements that cannot be found in other works of mission studies. An evangelical perspective characterizes entries in the *Evangelical Dictionary of World Missions*, edited by A. Scott Moreau, Harold Netland and Charles Van Engen (Baker and Paternoster, 2000). However, the material of this dictionary does not limit itself to evangelical missionary activity but has a wider and truly ecumenical scope.

The second edition of the *World Christian Encyclopedia*, edited by David Barrett (Oxford University Press, 2001), is a massive work in three volumes and is the kind of book every library should have. It is more extensive than anything attempted before, providing items such as a record of the current global status of Christianity and religions, a survey of peoples and languages of the world, a large section on methodology, an atlas, an article for each country of the world including data about the history and status of religions and Christianity, statistics and tables about churches and denominations, and much more. The thrust of the book is missiological, and the information provided is arranged in a helpful way for readers interested in taking part in Christian mission today. Based on this kind of data and on a databank of their own, Patrick Johnstone, Robin Johnstone, Jason Mandryk and a team have published *Operation World* (Paternoster Lifestyle, 2001). In its 798 pages these authors have condensed information similar to that provided by Barrett's book but arranged in a way that invites informed prayer each day of the year, individually, with the family or in church. Thus it is a typical missionary book in the best evangelical tradition that puts together scholarship, information and piety.

HISTORY

Evangelicals enthusiastic for missions have not always taken advantage of the great volume of historical material and wisdom available through a basic acquaintance with missions history. Among the bibliographical sources for the brief historical outline offered in chapter two, I mentioned classics such as Kenneth Scott Latourette's *History of the Expansion of Christianity* in seven volumes, now out of print (Harper, 1937-1944); this work has an incredible amount of data which still can be processed to understand unexplored aspects of mission history. The one-volume work of Stephen Neill, *A History of Christian Missions* (rev. ed.; Penguin, 1986), is a highly readable and helpful overview that may be complemented by the more popular, didactic, one-volume evangelical summary by Ruth A. Tucker, *From Jerusalem to Irian Jaya: A Biographical History of Christian Missions* (Zondervan, 1983). Tucker has also written an excellent overview of the involvement of women in missions, *Guardians of the Great Commission* (Zondervan, 1988), an area hardly touched on in the other overviews mentioned here. Restraints of time and space prevent the mention of some valuable historical material on missions in different regions of the world published in recent years. Instead, I limit myself to works of a more general scope.

For the twentieth century the best one-volume treatment is the work of Timothy Yates, *Christian Mission in the Twentieth Century* (Cambridge University Press, 1994), a book that offers a vast amount of informative material arranged and interpreted in a readable way. This is especially helpful for evangelicals who may not be acquainted with the missionary work and missiological reflection from mainline Protestant denominations and the ecumenical movement related to the World Council of Churches and the International Missionary Council.

One source of clues to aid the understanding of evangelical missionary activity from the United States, which dominated the second part of the twentieth century, is the symposium *Earthen Vessels: American Evangelicals and Foreign Missions 1880-1980,* edited by Joel Carpenter and Wilbert Shenk (Eerdmans, 1990). Much has been learned in recent years by the application of social sciences to writing and interpreting history, a perspective from which Brian Stanley approaches missionary activity from the U.K. in *The Bible and the Flag* (Inter-Varsity Press, 1990). Along the same lines Dana L. Robert wrote *American Women in Mission: A Social History of Their Thought and Practice* (Mercer University Press, 1996), a model of missiological research and interpretation.

Breadth and depth of perspective based on familiarity with historical facts and firm convictions about the missionary nature of the church characterizes the work of Andrew F. Walls, especially the material collected in *The Missionary Movement in Christian History: Studies in the Transmission of the Faith* (T & T Clark and Orbis, 1996) and *The Cross-Cultural Process in Christian History* (Orbis, 2002). Walls has been a pioneer in the use of interpretative keys for the history of missions that take seriously the present global nature of Christianity. The convergence of theology, history and cultural analysis, in the best missiological fashion, also characterizes the work of African missiologist Lamin Sanneh in his books *Translating the Message: The Missionary Impact on Culture* (Orbis, 1989) and *Encountering the West: Christianity and the Global Cultural Process: The African Dimension* (Orbis, 1993).

BIBLICAL BASIS

In previous chapters we have considered the specific effort in evangelical mission studies to search for New Testament patterns, in order to correct and illuminate contemporary mission activity. A helpful systematic contribution that focuses on evangelism and the New Testament comes from Michael Green, *Evangelism in the Early Church* (Eerdmans, 1970); this book summarizes the findings of contemporary scholarship from the perspective of an evangelist. A valuable complement with insights from the social sciences that are especially helpful for those interested in transcultural mission would be Derek Tidball, *An Introduction to the Sociology of the New Testament* (Paternoster, 1983). However, the biblical basis for mission has to be established in reference to the totality of the biblical message. It is necessary to correct the tendency to base mission on a few selected texts from the New Testament. What has to be grasped is God's purpose for humankind as revealed in Scripture, and the missionary thrust of the whole history of salvation. This will throw new light on the nature of mission.

Missiologist David Bosch pointed out in 1993 that in spite of the Protestant emphasis on the Bible, during the 1980s Catholic biblical scholars were by and large taking the missionary dimension of Scripture more seriously than their Protestant counterparts.[1] Two books could be considered a proof of Bosch's statement at that point: *Unity and Plurality: Mission in the Bible* (Orbis, 1990), written by Lucien Legrand, a French priest who had been a missionary in India since 1953; and the joint work of two American biblical scholars, Donald Senior and Carroll Stühlmueller, *The Biblical Foundations for Mission* (Orbis, 1983). The evangelical reader will notice that in the handling of biblical material from the Old and New Testaments these Catholic authors pay attention to critical issues which evangelical authors tend to overlook. Sometimes dealing with critical questions is necessary in order to take into account the totality of biblical revelation.

When the twenty-first century started, evangelical scholarship produced a new crop of valuable texts. From Walter C. Kaiser Jr. we have *Mission in the Old Testament: Israel as a Light to the Nations* (Baker, 2000), a clear and persuasive introduction to the Old Testament material. Then three volumes evidenced the current interest in the subject among evangelical scholars from the English-speaking world. *Salvation to the Ends of the Earth: A Biblical Theology of Mission*, with a short section on the Old Testament, was coauthored by Andreas J. Köstenberger and Peter T. O'Brien (InterVarsity Press, 2001); William F. Larkin and J. F. Williams edited *Mission in the New Testament: An Evangelical Approach*, published in the series sponsored by the American Society of Missiology (Orbis, 1998); and Peter Bolt and Mark Thompson edited a fresh and varied treatment by twenty-five authors of the apostle Paul's mission and his writings, *The Gospel to the Nations: Perspectives on Paul's Mission* (InterVarsity Press, 2000).

Four more books may be placed in this section because, though their authors offer a more systematic theological approach with a holistic agenda, they deal with it on the basis of careful examination of the biblical material. A classical treatment of some key issues that surfaced in the Lausanne movement was written by John R. W. Stott in *Christian Mission in the Modern World* (InterVarsity Press, 1975). A strong trinitarian emphasis that reflects a life of missionary experience is the distinctive mark of Lesslie Newbigin, *The Open Secret* (rev. ed.; Eerdmans, 1995). C. René Padilla's *Mission Between the Times* (Eerdmans, 1985) is a polemical stance offering perspectives from churches that are the result of evangelical mission work. And key biblical motifs were developed by Orlando Costas as a basis for his posthumous book *Liberating News: A Theology of Contextual Evangelization* (Eerdmans, 1989).

MISSION THEOLOGY

A helpful panorama of the development of mission theology is provided by the late South African missiologist David Bosch in his massive overview, *Transforming Mission: Paradigm Shifts in Theology of Mission* (Orbis, 1991). Bosch processed a huge amount of information in the different disciplines that relate to mission studies, arranging it in a sequence that follows the cultural shifts that author Thomas Kuhn has identified as paradigm shifts in the Western world. Bosch shows how different paradigms have influenced the way Christian mission has been conceived and executed. The first quarter of his book deals with New Testament models of mission and provides a perceptive summary of twentieth-century studies on biblical mission theology. As a companion to Bosch's book, Norman E. Thomas has compiled a source book, *Classic Texts in Mission and World Christianity* (Orbis, 1995). Following a chronological approach, a quarter of the book is dedicated to the first eighteen centuries of Christian history and three-quarters to the more recent two hundred years.

Three older overviews are still useful for understanding contemporary mission theology. Rodger C. Bassham, *Mission Theology 1948-1975: Years of Worldwide Creative Tension, Ecumenical, Evangelical and Roman Catholic* (William Carey Library, 1979), gives special attention to the debates and dialogues in the years that preceded the Lausanne movement. James A. Scherer is a Lutheran missiologist who summarizes developments in the Catholic, ecumenical Protestant and evangelical movements in *Gospel, Church and Kingdom: Comparative Studies in World Mission Theology* (Augsburg, 1987). Arthur F. Glasser with Donald A. McGavran summarizes the more conservative perspective in *Contemporary Theologies of Mission* (Baker, 1983). These overviews do not limit themselves to theology but offer sound historical background, grounding theological reflection in the processes of missionary activity, organization, consultation and dialogue that have been taking place in a variety of missiological foci. A wide variety of authors contributed chapters to a more recent symposium, *The Good News of the Kingdom: Mission Theology in the Third Millennium*, edited by Charles Van Engen, Dean S. Gilliland and Paul Pierson (Orbis, 1993). John Stott, who has played a significant role in the missiological dialogue within the Lausanne movement, offers the basic contours of an evangelical theology of mission in his book *The Contemporary Christian* (InterVarsity Press, 1992). An ecumenical overview of contemporary missionary theology can be found in *Missiology: An Ecumenical Introduction. Texts and Contexts of Global Christianity*, edited by F. J. Verstraelen, A. Camps, L. A. Hoedemaker and M. R. Spindler (Eerdmans, 1995).

Some collective volumes have kept a record of the global dialogue that has been taking place among evangelical theologians of the Third World, with special reference to the relation between Christian mission and social transformation. Most of the writers are not primarily scholars but practitioners of mission in Asia, Africa and Latin America. At stake every day in their ministry within those regions, or in the ghettos of North American cities, is their credibility as messengers of Jesus Christ. Thus, some questions of the renewed Christology essential for mission are found in *Sharing Jesus in the Two Thirds World* (Eerdmans, 1983), and some of the practical and theological questions involved in responding to human need are explored in *The Church in Response to Human Need* (Eerdmans, 1987), both edited by Vinay Samuel and Chris Sugden. A recent addition to this series, also edited by Samuel and Sugden, is *Mission as Transformation: A Theology of the Whole Gospel* (Regnum, 1999), which develops material gathered since 1983.

Lesslie Newbigin, already much referred to in this book, was one of the most respected voices in mission theology during the last part of the twentieth century. He focused attention particularly on the need to evangelize the West. Exploring what it would take for the church to adopt again a missionary stance in Western societies, Newbigin dedicated great energy to a critical appraisal of modernity and the Enlightenment. A summary of his argument may be found in his books *The Gospel in a Pluralist Society* (Eerdmans, 1989) and *Truth to Tell: The Gospel as Public Truth* (Eerdmans, 1991).

Vinoth Ramachandra, an evangelical missiologist from Sri Lanka, has made creative use of Newbigin's insights in his book *The Recovery of Mission: Beyond the Pluralist Paradigm* (Eerdmans and Paternoster, 1996), which deals critically with Newbigin and three other Asian theologians of mission. Ramachandra not only takes us beyond the pluralist paradigm but also develops a well-argued evangelistic and missionary proposal for our time.

Newbigin's insight that the gospel is public truth and not just private opinion has been taken on by Kwame Bediako, an African missiologist developing a mission theology that uses the basic tenets of the Christian faith to interpret the social and cultural reality of Africa in the twenty-first century, within the framework of a truly world Christian church whose center of gravity has moved southward. In his book *Christianity in Africa: The Renewal of a Non-Western Religion* (Edinburgh University Press and Orbis, 1995), Bediako also takes cues from Andrew Walls.

With the background of missionary experience in Asia and specialization in Old Testament studies, Chris Wright offers a comprehensive analysis of pluralism in his book *Thinking Clearly About the Uniqueness of Jesus* (Monarch, 1997).

As the church in the West regains a missionary stance, mission theology has to respond to the kind of pluralism that has become the cultural and spiritual milieu of contemporary societies. Newbigin's agenda was also taken up by the Gospel and Culture movement in North America and Europe, and a good sample of the ongoing reflection is *The Church Between Gospel and Culture: The Emerging Mission in North America*, edited by Craig Van Gelder and George H. Hunsberger (Eerdmans, 1996). Although ecclesiology used to be a weak point of evangelical theology, recently some valuable studies have been developed with a missiological emphasis. Charles Van Engen develops classic patristic statements and Reformation teaching about the nature of the church into a missional ecclesiology in his highly didactic *God's Missionary People: Rethinking the Purpose of the Local Church* (Baker, 1991). Howard Snyder makes a valuable contribution to missional ecclesiology, paying special attention to the way church structures are affected by revivals and missionary advance, in his books *Radical Renewal: The Problem of Wineskins Today* (rev. ed.; Touch, 1996) and *Liberating the Church: The Ecology of Church & Kingdom* (InterVarsity, 1982).

CRITICAL ISSUES AND A PROMISE

Commitment to missionary obedience has brought a critical approach from some missiologists. Christian mission came under attack from secularist social scientists and radical theologians, especially after World War II, and some of the historical books mentioned in this chapter offer good accounts of that critical process. Although this type of criticism may be painful at times, alert missiologists have learned from it. However, more may be learned from the self-criticism of those missiologists who have missionary experience and are not writing from a purely academic stance. A critical study of the financial aspects of Western missionary work may be found in Jonathan J. Bonk, *Missions and Money: Affluence as a Western Missionary Problem* (Orbis, 1991). The failures in the relationships between evangelical mission-minded practitioners and scholars on the one hand, and social scientists on the other has been well studied by anthropologist Charles R. Taber in his book *To Understand the World, to Save the World* (Trinity Press International, 2000), which offers guidelines for the interface between missiology and the social sciences. Missiologists James F. Engel and William A. Dyrness have sounded a critical note of alarm about the future of the American missionary enterprise in their book *Changing the Mind of Missions: Where Have We Gone Wrong?* (InterVarsity Press, 2000).

Several of the international evangelical authors mentioned in this list have participated in events sponsored by the Missions Commission of the World Evangelical Fellowship. A good sample of their most recent work is a book that could well be an introductory textbook to mission studies, *Global Missiology for the 21st Century: The Iguassu Dialogue*, edited by William D. Taylor (Baker, 2000). As the subtitle indicates, the book is the result of the October 1999 Iguassu Missiological Consultation held in Brazil. Forty-one writers contributed to it, and the book reflects not only material specially commissioned for the event but also the lively dialogue that took place. The book is evidence that the evangelical missionary vision and enthusiasm characteristic of the twentieth century has not waned but has now taken on a global dimension.

Notes

Chapter 1: Christian Mission in a New Century

[1]Helpful statistical data about mission may be found in Bryant L. Myers, *The New Context of World Mission* (MARC, 1996); and in Patrick Johnstone, Robin Johnstone and Jason Mandryk, *Operation World*, 6th ed. (Paternoster Lifestyle, 2001).

[2]Andrew Walls, "Culture and Coherence in Christian History," *Evangelical Review of Theology* 9, no. 3 (1984): 215.

[3]Walbert Bühlman, *The Church of the Future* (Orbis, 1986), p. 6.

[4]Robert Mapes Anderson, *Vision of the Disinherited: The Making of American Pentecostalism* (Oxford University Press, 1979).

[5]Roland Allen, *The Spontaneous Expansion of the Church and the Causes That Hinder It* (World Dominion, 1927).

[6]Lesslie Newbigin, *Foolishness to the Greeks: The Gospel and Western Culture* (Eerdmans, 1986), p. 3.

[7]David Bosch, "Reflections on Biblical Models of Mission," in *Towards the 21st Century in Christian Mission*, ed. James M. Phillips and Robert T. Coote (Eerdmans, 1993), p. 177.

[8]I take the phrase from Brazilian theologian Valdir R. Steuernagel, *Obediencia missionária e prática histórica: Em busca de modelos (Missionary Obedience and Historical Practice: In Search of Models)* (ABU Editora, 1993).

[9]Eugene A. Nida, *Message and Mission: The Communication of the Christian Faith*, rev. ed. (William Carey Library, 1990); Jacob A. Loewen, *Culture and Human Values: Christian Intervention in Anthropological Perspective* (William Carey Library, 1975); Charles Taber, *The World Is Too Much with Us: Culture in Modern Protestant Missions* (Mercer University Press, 1991); Paul G. Hiebert, *Anthropological Insights for Missionaries* (Baker, 1985); Miriam Adeney, *God's Foreign Policy* (Eerdmans, 1984).

[10]Stott presented the Bible expositions about the Great Commission that afterward became highly influential. C. F. Henry and W. S. Mooneyham, eds., *One Race, One Gospel, One Task* (World Wide, 1967). For an updated summary of Stott's Christology of mission see his book *The Contemporary Christian* (InterVarsity Press, 1992), pp. 356-74.

[11]See the excellent work done along these lines by Mortimer Arias, *The Great Commission* (Abingdon, 1992).

[12]Samuel Escobar, "Evangelism and Man's Search for Freedom, Justice and Fulfillment," in *Let the Earth Hear His Voice*, ed. J. D. Douglas (World Wide, 1975), pp. 303-27.

[13]C. René Padilla, "Evangelism and the World," in *Let the Earth Hear His Voice*, ed. J. D. Douglas (World Wide, 1975), pp. 116-46.

Chapter 2: Mud and Glory

[1] Annual statistical update by David Barrett, *International Bulletin of Missionary Research* 24, no. 1 (2000): 25.

[2] I have dealt more extensively with authors and questions in this section in my article "Mission Studies Past, Present and Future," *Missiology* 24, no. 1 (1996): 3-29.

[3] Eduardo Hoornaert, *The Memory of the Christian People* (Orbis, 1988), p. xii.

[4] Ibid., pp. 13-14.

[5] Ibid., pp. 176-77.

[6] Ruth Tucker, *Guardians of the Great Commission* (Zondervan, 1988), p. 9.

[7] Ruth Tucker, "Female Mission Strategists: A Historical and Contemporary Perspective," *Missiology* 15, no. 1 (1987): 76.

[8] Tucker, *Guardians*, p. 195.

[9] Kenneth Scott Latourette, *The Unquenchable Light* (Eyre & Spottiswoode, 1948), pp. ix-x.

[10] Ralph D. Winter, *The Twenty-Five Unbelievable Years, 1945 to 1969* (William Carey Library, 1970).

[11] Tom Houston, based on data by David Barrett, "Scenario 2000: World Evangelization Review," in *Mission at the Dawn of the 21st Century*, ed. Paul Varo Martinson (Kirk House, 1999), p. 372.

[12] Andrew Walls, "The Mission of the Church Today in the Light of Global History," in *Mission at the Dawn of the 21st Century*, ed. Paul Varo Martinson (Kirk House, 1999), p. 385.

[13] Henry J. Cadbury, *The Book of Acts in History* (Harper, 1955), p. 58.

[14] For a brief and clear summary of this process see F. F. Bruce, *First Century Faith*, rev. ed. (InterVarsity Press, 1977).

[15] Justo L. González, *Historia de las misiones (History of Missions)* (La Aurora, 1970).

[16] From Gregory's *Panegyric*, quoted in Alan Kreider, *The Change of Conversion and the Origin of Christendom* (Trinity Press International, 1999), p. 29.

[17] Gustavo Gutiérrez, *Las Casas: In Search of the Poor of Jesus Christ* (Orbis, 1993), pp. 139-40.

[18] Ibid., p. 143.

[19] Latourette, *Unquenchable Light*, pp. 42-43.

[20] Two Spanish historians, Margarita Cantera and Santiago Cantera, have provided a valuable summary of this process in their *Los monjes y la cristianización de Europa (Monks and the Christianization of Europe)* (Arco Libros, 1996).

[21] Latourette, *Unquenchable Light*, p. 44.

[22] Stephen Neill, *A History of Christian Missions* (Penguin, 1986), pp. 99-100.

[23] Ibid., pp. 114-15.

[24] Ibid., pp. 116-17.

[25] Gutiérrez's book *Las Casas* is a thorough study of Las Casas and the theological debates among missionaries and theologians of the sixteenth century.

[26] Mario A. Rodriguez León, "Invasion and Evangelization in the Sixteenth Century," in *The Church in Latin America 1492-1992*, ed. Enrique Dussel (Burns & Oates, Orbis, 1992), pp. 44-45.

[27] Ibid., p. 53.

[28] Robert Bolton, *The Mission* (Jove, 1986).

[29]Roger Mehl, *The Sociology of Protestantism* (SCM Press, 1970), p. 166.

[30]Andrew Walls, "The American Dimension in the History of the Missionary Movement," in *Earthen Vessels: American Evangelicals and Foreign Missions*, ed. Joel A. Carpenter and Wilbert R. Shenk (Eerdmans, 1990), p. 15.

[31]Dana L. Robert, "The Origin of the Student Volunteer Watchword: 'The Evangelization of the World in This Generation,'" *International Bulletin of Missionary Research* 10, no. 4 (1986): 186.

[32]Ada Lum, *A Hitchhiker's Guide to Missions* (InterVarsity Press, 1984). For a history of the International Fellowship of Evangelical Students see Peter Lowman, *The Day of His Power* (InterVarsity Press, 1983).

[33]Mehl, *Sociology of Protestantism*, pp. 66-67.

Chapter 3: A Brave New World Order

[1]Robert J. Schreiter, *The New Catholicity* (Orbis, 1997), p. 6.

[2]Jacques Attali, *Millennium* (Times, 1991), pp. 8-9.

[3]Howard A. Snyder, *Earthcurrents: The Struggle for the World's Soul* (Abingdon, 1995), p. 46.

[4]Schreiter, *New Catholicity*, p. 9.

[5]Ibid.

[6]C. René Padilla, *Mission Between the Times* (Eerdmans, 1985), pp. 16-17.

[7]Lamin Sanneh, *Translating the Message: The Missionary Impact on Culture* (Orbis, 1989), p. 2.

[8]Ibid., p. 138.

[9]Justo L. González, *For the Healing of the Nations* (Orbis, 1999), p. 78.

[10]Ibid., p. 79.

[11]Howard A. Snyder, ed., *Global Good News* (Abingdon, 2001), p. 224.

[12]Joseph D. Souza, "The Saffronization Challenge," in *Global Missiology for the 21st Century: The Iguassu Dialogue*, ed. William D. Taylor (Baker, 2000).

[13]Schreiter, *New Catholicity*, p. 7.

[14]Peter F. Drucker, "The Age of Social Transformation," *Atlantic Monthly*, November 1994, p. 73 (emphasis mine).

[15]Agencies such as World Vision, MAP, Food for the Hungry, Habitat for Humanity, MEDA and World Concern have grown significantly in recent years. Several volumes in the series Cases in Holistic Ministry from MARC (World Vision International) provide a helpful overview.

[16]Tim Stafford, "The Criminologist Who Discovered Churches," *Christianity Today*, June 14, 1999, pp. 35-39.

[17]Cecilia Mariz, *Coping with Poverty* (Temple University Press, 1994).

[18]David Martin, *Tongues of Fire* (Basil Blackwell, 1990). Martin uses studies about Pentecostal growth in South Africa and South Korea for comparison with his massive study about Latin America.

[19]Snyder, *Global Good News*, p. 224.

Chapter 4: Post-Christian and Postmodern

[1]Roger Mehl, *Sociology of Protestantism* (Westminster Press, 1970), p. 67.

[2]Kenneth Scott Latourette, *The Christian Outlook* (Harper & Brothers, 1948), p. 8.

[3]The title of a very helpful book by Stanley Hauerwas and William H. Willimon, which deals

with the issue in the U.S. context: *Resident Aliens* (Abingdon, 1989).

[4]Rosemary Dowsett, "Dry Bones in the West," in *Global Missiology for the 21st Century: The Iguassu Dialogue*, ed. William D. Taylor (Baker, 2000), p. 449.

[5]Jacques Attali, *Millennium* (Times, 1991), p. 5.

[6]Michael Green, *Evangelism in the Early Church* (Eerdmans, 1970).

[7]Helpful at this point is the article by John W. Drane, "Methods and Perspectives in Understanding the New Age," *Themelios* 23, no. 2 (1998): 22-34.

[8]Jim Pluedemann, "Spiritual Formation," in *Evangelical Dictionary of World Missions,* ed. A. Scott Moreau, Harold Netland and Charles Van Engen (Baker, Paternoster, 2000), p. 902.

[9]Ibid.

[10]George Hunter III, "The Case for Culturally Relevant Congregations," in *Global Good News,* ed. Howard Snyder (Abingdon, 2001), p. 105.

[11]For a recent evaluation of some modern theological work on religions see Vinoth Ramachandra, *The Recovery of Mission* (Eerdmans, Paternoster, 1996).

[12]Rev. G. Penny Nixon, "Letter to the Editor," *Urbana Today,* December 30, 1990, p. 4.

[13]Carl F. H. Henry, *Evangelical Responsibility in Contemporary Theology* (Eerdmans, 1957), pp. 43, 33.

[14]"The Willowbank Report on Gospel and Culture," in *Making Christ Known: Historic Mission Documents from the Lausanne Movement 1974-1989,* ed. John R. W. Stott (Eerdmans, Paternoster, 1996), p. 88.

[15]Ibid., p. 89.

Chapter 5: We Believe in a Missionary God

[1]Vishal Mangalwadi, *Missionary Conspiracy: Letters to a Postmodern Hindu* (OM, 1998), pp. 23, 20.

[2]Lesslie Newbigin, *The Gospel in a Pluralist Society* (SPCK, 1989), pp. 882-83.

[3]Lucien Legrand, *Unity and Plurality: Mission in the Bible* (Orbis, 1990), p. xiv.

[4]Ibid., p. 4.

[5]Walter C. Kaiser Jr., *Mission in the Old Testament: Israel as a Light to the Nations* (Baker, 2000), pp. 30-33.

[6]Legrand, *Unity and Plurality,* pp. 15-18.

[7]Justo L. González, *Acts: The Gospel of the Spirit* (Orbis, 2001), p. 161.

Chapter 6: Christ: God's Best Missionary

[1]Vishal Mangalwadi, *Missionary Conspiracy: Letters to a Postmodern Hindu* (OM, 1998), p. 10.

[2]John R. W. Stott, ed., *Making Christ Known: Historic Mission Documents from the Lausanne Movement 1974-1989* (Eerdmans, Paternoster, 1996), p. 234.

[3]Vinoth Ramachandra, *The Recovery of Mission* (Eerdmans, Paternoster, 1996), p. 180.

[4]Howard Snyder, ed., *Global Good News* (Abingdon, 2001), p. 222.

[5]John R. W. Stott, *The Contemporary Christian* (InterVarsity Press, 1992), p. 57.

[6]Alister E. McGrath, *Evangelicalism and the Future of Christianity* (InterVarsity Press, 1995), p. 65.

[7]The Evangelical-Roman Catholic Dialogue on Mission (ERCDOM) was a process that took

place in three sessions (Venice, 1977; Cambridge, 1982; and Landevennec, France, 1984).

[8]Basil Meeking and John R. W. Stott, eds., *The Evangelical-Roman Catholic Dialogue on Mission 1978-1987* (Paternoster, Eerdmans, 1988), (emphasis mine).

[9]"The Hong Kong Call to Conversion," *Evangelical Review of Theology* 16, no. 3 (1992): 264.

[10]Ibid., pp. 264-65.

[11]C. René Padilla, "Bible Studies," *Missiology* 10, no. 3 (1982): 319-38.

[12]John R. W. Stott, "The Christology of Mission," in *The Contemporary Christian*, p. 357.

[13]Ibid., p. 358.

[14]Viv Grigg, *Companion to the Poor* (MARC, 1990).

[15]See, for instance, C. René Padilla, ed., *The New Face of Evangelicalism: An International Symposium on the Lausanne Covenant* (InterVarsity Press, 1976); Vinay Samuel and Chris Sugden, eds., *Sharing Jesus in the Two Thirds World* (Eerdmans, 1983).

[16]In Samuel and Sugden, *Sharing Jesus*, p. 28.

[17]Ramachandra, *Recovery of Mission*, p. 196.

Chapter 7: The Holy Spirit and Christian Mission

[1]John V. Taylor, *The Go-Between God: The Holy Spirit and Christian Mission* (Fortress, 1973), p. 3.

[2]David B. Barrett, "Statistics, Global," in *Dictionary of Pentecostal and Charismatic Movements*, ed. Stanley M. Burgess, Gary B. McGee and Patrick H. Alexander (Zondervan, 1988), pp. 810-30.

[3]Gary McGee, "Initial Evidence: A Biblical Perspective," in *Dictionary of Pentecostal and Charismatic Movements*, ed. Stanley M. Burgess, Gary B. McGee and Patrick H. Alexander (Zondervan, 1988), p. 455.

[4]J. B. A. Kessler, *A Study of the Older Protestant Missions and Churches in Peru and Chile* (Goes, Oosterbaan & Le Cointre, 1967), chaps. 8, 9, 21.

[5]Gary McGee, "Melvin Lyle Hodges," in *Biographical Dictionary of Christian Missions*, ed. Gerald H. Anderson (Simon & Schuster, Macmillan, 1998), p. 296.

[6]Charles H. Long and Anne Rowthorn, "The Missionary Legacy of Roland Allen," in *Mission Legacies*, ed. Gerald H. Anderson, Robert T. Coote, Norman A. Horner and James M. Phillips (Orbis, 1994), pp. 383-90.

[7]Russell P. Spittler, "Implicit Values in Pentecostal Missions," *Missiology* 16, no. 4 (1988): 416.

[8]In relation to this point I have studied the case of Latin America with more detail in my book *Changing Tides* (Orbis, 2002).

[9]Lesslie Newbigin, *The Household of Faith* (Friendship, 1954), p. 122.

[10]I think of Harry R. Boer, *Pentecost and Missions*; John V. Taylor, *The Go-Between God*; several works of James D. G. Dunn; and more recently Gordon Fee, *God's Empowering Presence* (Hendrickson, 1994).

[11]John Stott, *Evangelical Truth* (InterVarsity Press, 1999), p. 104.

[12]Ajith Fernando, "The Holy Spirit, the Divine Implementer of Mission," in *Global Missiology for the 21st Century: The Iguassu Dialogue*, ed. William D. Taylor (Baker, 2000), p. 225.

[13]Harry R. Boer, *Pentecost and Missions* (Eerdmans, 1979), p. 71.

[14]Ibid., p. 133.

[15]Roland Allen, "The Spirit, the Source and Test of New Forms of Missionary Activity," selection from *Pentecost and the World: The Revelation of the Holy Spirit in the Acts of the Apostles* (1917), in *The Holy Spirit and Mission Dynamics,* ed. Douglas McConnell (William Carey Library, 1997), p. 96.

[16]Emil Brunner, *The Misunderstanding of the Church* (Westminster Press, 1953), p. 47.

[17]Ibid.

[18]Valdir R. Steuernagel, *Obediencia missionária e prática histórica: Em busca de modelos (Missionary Obedience and Historical Practice: In Search for Models)* (ABU Editora, 1993).

Chapter 8: Text and Context: The Word Through New Eyes

[1]A. M. Chirgwin, *The Bible in World Evangelism* (Friendship, 1954), p. 47.

[2]Ibid., p. 34.

[3]Stephen Neill, *A History of Christian Missions,* rev. ed. (Penguin, 1986), p. 177.

[4]José Míguez Bonino, "Main Currents of Protestantism," in *Integration of Man and Society in Latin America,* ed. Samuel Shapiro (Notre Dame University Press, 1967), p. 193.

[5]Bernard Ramm, *Protestant Biblical Interpretation* (Baker, 1970), p. 55.

[6]Chirgwin, *Bible in World Evangelism,* p. 39.

[7]John A. Mackay, *Christianity on the Frontier* (Macmillan, 1950), p. 117.

[8]Lamin Sanneh, *Translating the Message: The Missionary Impact on Culture* (Orbis, 1989), p. 4.

[9]Kwame Bediako, *Christianity in Africa: The Renewal of a Non-Western Religion* (Edinburgh University Press, Orbis, 1995), pp. 154-56.

[10]Roland Allen, *Missionary Methods; St. Paul's or Ours?* (World Dominion, 1962).

[11]Ibid., p. 55.

[12]Ibid., p. 62.

[13]Andrew F. Walls, "Culture and Coherence in Christian History," *Evangelical Review of Theology* 9, no. 3 (1985): 222.

[14]David B. Barrett, *Schism and Renewal in Africa* (Oxford University Press, 1968), pp. 127, 129.

[15]John R. W. Stott, "The Authority and Power of the Bible," in *The New Face of Evangelicalism: An International Symposium on the Lausanne Covenant,* ed. C. René Padilla (InterVarsity Press, 1976), pp. 44-45.

[16]Lorenzo Bautista, Hidalgo B. Garcia and Sze-Kar Wan, "The Asian Way of Thinking in Theology," *Evangelical Review of Theology* 6, no. 1 (1982): 61.

[17]Ibid., p. 41.

[18]Ibid., p. 49.

[19]David Gitari, "The Claims of Jesus Christ in the African Context," *Evangelical Review of Theology* 6, no. 2 (1982): 215.

[20]Ibid., p. 119.

[21]Ibid., pp. 220-21.

Chapter 9: Misson as Transforming Service

[1]Blanca Muratorio, *Etnicidad, evangelización y protesta en el Ecuador (Ethnicity, Evangelization and Protest in Ecuador)* (CIESE, 1981), pp. 73-98.

[2]I offered a brief account of this process in my presentation at the Lausanne Congress on

World Evangelization, "Evangelism and Man's Search for Freedom, Justice and Fulfillment," in *Let the Earth Hear His Voice*, ed. J. D. Douglas (World Wide, 1975), pp. 303-18.

[3]Michael Cassidy, "The Ethics of Political Nationalism," in *One Race, One Gospel, One Task*, ed. C. F. H. Henry and W. S. Mooneyham (World Wide, 1967), 2:312-16.

[4]Leighton Ford, "The Church and Evangelism in a Day of Revolution," in *Evangelism Now*, ed. George M. Wilson (World Wide, 1970), p. 62.

[5]Samuel Escobar, "The Social Impact of the Gospel," in *Is Revolution Change?* ed. Brian Griffiths (Inter-Varsity Press, 1972), pp. 100, 98.

[6]Benjamin E. Fernando, "The Evangel and Social Upheaval (part 2)," in *Christ Seeks Asia*, ed. W. S. Mooneyham (Rock House, 1969), pp. 118-19.

[7]Michael Green, *Evangelism in the Early Church* (Hodder & Stoughton, 1970), p. 165.

[8]André Biéler, *The Social Humanism of Calvin* (John Knox Press, 1964), pp. 28-29.

[9]H. W. Beyer, in *Theological Dictionary of the New Testament*, ed. G. Kittel (Eerdmans, 1968), 2:82.

[10]Ibid., p. 84.

[11]"The Grand Rapids Report on Evangelism and Social Responsibility: An Evangelical Commitment," in *Making Christ Known: Historic Mission Documents from the Lausanne Movement 1974-1989*, ed. John R. W. Stott (Eerdmans, Paternoster, 1996), p. 185.

[12]Ibid., p. 178.

[13]Ibid., p. 181.

[14]Ibid., p. 182.

Chapter 10: A New Way of Looking at the World

[1]Daniel E. Fountain, *Health, the Bible and the Church* (Billy Graham Center, 1989), p. 42.

[2]Ibid.

[3]F. F. Bruce, *I and II Corinthians*, New Century Bible Commentary (Eerdmans, 1987), p. 208.

[4]Fountain, *Health*, p. 12.

[5]Ibid., p. 41.

[6]Ibid., p. 31.

[7]Ajith Fernando, "The Church: The Mirror of the Trinity," in *Global Missiology for the 21st Century: The Iguassu Dialogue*, ed. William D. Taylor (Baker, 2000), p. 248.

[8]Charles H. Kraft, *Christianity with Power: Your Worldview and Your Experience of the Supernatural* (Servant, 1989).

[9]Ibid., p. 4.

[10]Ibid., p. 29.

[11]Lesslie Newbigin, *Foolishness to the Greeks: The Gospel and Western Culture* (Eerdmans, 1986), p. 3.

[12]Ibid., p. 2.

[13]Ibid., pp. 2-3.

[14]Ibid., p. 45.

[15]David A. Shank, *What Western Christians Can Learn from African-Initiated Churches* (Mennonite Board of Missions, 2000), p. 1.

[16]Ibid., p. 4.

[17]Ibid., pp. 4-11.

[18]Larry Pate, *From Every People* (MARC, 1989), p. 5.

[19]Ibid., p. 19.

[20]Ted Limpic, *Catálogo de organizaciones misioneras iberoamericanas (Catalog of Iberoamerican Missionary Organizations)* (Comibam, 1997), p. 19.

[21]Concerning this point see my book *Changing Tides* (Orbis, 2002).

[22]Paul G. Hiebert, "Missions and the Renewal of the Church," in *Exploring Church Growth*, ed. Wilbert R. Shenk (Eerdmans, 1983), p. 157.

[23]The development of "managerial missiology" and some of the features I comment on here may be seen in the works of Peter Wagner, Ralph Winter, Luids Bush, George Otis and others like them. See my article "Evangelical Missiology: Peering into the Future at the Turn of the Century," in *Global Missiology for the 21st Century: The Iguassu Dialogue*, ed. William D. Taylor (Baker, 2000), pp. 101-22; and the response by David Tai-Woong Lee, pp. 133-48.

[24]C. René Padilla, *Mission Between the Times* (Eerdmans, 1985), p. 169.

[25]Ibid., p. 142 (author's emphasis).

[26]Justo L. González, *For the Healing of the Nations* (Orbis, 1999), p. 20.

[27]Ibid., p. 109.

Chapter 11: For Further Study

[1]David Bosch, "Reflections on Biblical Models of Mission," in *Towards the 21st Century in Christian Mission*, ed. James M. Phillips and Robert T. Coote (Eerdmans, 1993), p. 178.

Scripture Index

...to see majority world ...sincerely believe, dili-...and the Word of God. ...have helped burgeon-...*depth*. Three key pro-...le their congregations

...re than 120 major-...t the postgraduate ...grees, these church ...eneration of pastors

...stors for instruction ...nars provide inten-...n Bible exposition, ...hing.

...ries and Bible col-...d books to tens of thousands of pastors, many of whom before had nearly empty bookshelves.

You can participate in the global church. Find out more by visiting JSM at <www.johnstott.org> or contacting JSM at <info@johnstott.org>.